Blind Descent is an absolutely gripping, factual narrative of Brian Dickinson's extraordinary experience on Everest. The story of his descent just after losing his eyesight while low on oxygen kept me at the edge of my seat. This book is emotionally charged and so compelling that I found it all but impossible to put down. *Blind Descent* is a must-read!

DON D. MANN
SEAL Team Six

Who would have thought Mount Everest would now have two blind climbers? But I got the added pleasure of ascending the mountain blind as well. Brian's story is a harrowing adventure, a testament to his faith, and well worth the read. I only wish I'd known him before his climb so I could have given him some tips on descending by feel.

ERIK WEIHENMAYER
First blind climber to summit Mount Everest

Personal strength, Navy training, and family support got Brian Dickinson to the summit of Mount Everest. Yet when he found himself blind and alone atop the highest point on earth, it was Brian's faith that led the way down during his amazing and treacherous blind descent.

JIM DAVIDSON
Climber and coauthor of *The Ledge: An Inspirational Story of Friendship and Survival*

BLIND
DESCENT

Surviving Alone and Blind on Mount Everest

BLIND DESCENT

BRIAN DICKINSON

Tyndale House Publishers, Inc.
Carol Stream, Illinois

Visit Tyndale online at www.tyndale.com.

TYNDALE and Tyndale's quill logo are registered trademarks of Tyndale House Publishers, Inc.

Blind Descent: Surviving Alone and Blind on Mount Everest

Designed by Stephen Vosloo

Edited by Stephanie Rische

Published in association with the literary agency WTA Services LLC, Smyrna, TN.

Some of the names in this book have been changed out of respect for the privacy of the individuals mentioned.

ISBN 978-1-4143-9170-0 Hardcover
ISBN 978-1-4143-9862-4 ITPE edition

Printed in the United States of America

20	19	18	17	16	15	14
7	6	5	4	3	2	1

I'd like to dedicate this book to my wife, JoAnna, and my children, Emily and Jordan, who make life worth living. I couldn't ask for a more supportive and loving family.

CONTENTS

PROLOGUE

March 30, 2011

Snoqualmie, Washington

THE SKY was a menacing gunmetal gray, with dark storm clouds flowing in and casting an ominous shadow over the snowcapped peaks in the distance. This would have made for horrible climbing conditions, but it was an eerily fitting backdrop for what I was about to do.

The house was blanketed in silence. My wife, JoAnna, was at work, and our kids were both in school. I'd spent the past several weeks cramming in as much family time as possible, playing endless hours of LEGOs with Emily, who had just turned seven, and Jordan, who was four. Now it was finally time. I'd checked everything off my to-do list, and I had the house to myself. It was a moment I'd been thinking about and dreading for months.

In a matter of days, I would set off on my two-month expedition to Mount Everest. It wasn't the climbing that had me anxious—it was the thought of being away from my family for so long. When it came to the climb itself, I wasn't worried. I was in the best shape of my life, and I had planned everything down to the last detail. But I was also aware of the reality that people *do* die on Everest. No matter how well prepared you are, there are always things that are out of your control—extreme weather, shifting icefalls, avalanches, cerebral edema. Let's face it, there's a reason they call the top of Mount Everest the death zone.

As the winds picked up and rain began pelting my office window, I cast one last glance at the darkened face of Mount Si, which was slowly disappearing into the Washington mist. Then I sat down at my desk and powered up my MacBook. After I'd centered myself in the video frame, I took a deep breath and hit Record. I could already feel the tears burning behind my eyes.

"Hello, JoAnna," I began, a sob catching in my throat. "If you're watching this, something must have gone terribly wrong, and I'm in heaven now, watching you."

CHAPTER 1

EXPEDITION OF A LIFETIME

"I know the plans I have for you," declares the LORD, "plans to prosper you and not to harm you, plans to give you hope and a future."

JEREMIAH 29:11

GROWING UP in the small town of Rogue River, Oregon, I never imagined that one day I would be planning a Mount Everest expedition. My family and I lived in the shadow of the Siskiyou Mountains, and I'd heard plenty of news reports about mountaineering disasters—especially the ones that occurred on the highest peak in the world. I was just a kid in the 1980s, when more climbers began ascending above 26,000 feet on Everest. That translated to more fatalities— and more media coverage. Between 1980 and 2002, 91 climbers died during their attempt to summit.

In 1982 alone, tragedy struck expeditions from four different countries. British climbers Peter Boardman and Joe Tasker disappeared while attempting to be the first to climb the northeast ridge. Then a Canadian expedition lost their cameraman to an icefall, and just a few days later, three of their Sherpas lost their lives in an avalanche. The American team wasn't exempt from tragedy that year either, as a woman named Marty Hoey, who was expected to become the first woman from the United States to summit Everest, fell to her death. Even a veteran Everest climber from Japan and his climbing partner died near the summit due to extreme weather before the year came to a close.[1]

And then, more than a decade later, disaster struck again when eight people were caught in a blizzard and died on Everest. Over the course of the 1996 season, 15 people died trying to reach the summit, making it Everest's deadliest year in history.[2]

As a child and a young adult, I was gripped by those stories, but it seemed insane to me that mountaineers would climb in such arctic and oxygen-deprived conditions. Why would people want to risk plummeting to their death or losing body parts to frostbite? Like most people, I was a victim of the media. Although only 2 to 3 percent of those who attempted to summit Everest lost their lives, the news seemed to report only the fatalities. Everest seemed like an impossible death trap that only a few elite individuals could conquer. And even then, they'd remain permanently damaged—physically or mentally—as a result of the experience.

But while I may not have had visions of climbing the tallest peak in the world one day, I was a very daring kid. I started participating in extreme sports as soon as I was old enough to venture out without supervision. Now that I'm a parent myself, I realize how much stress I put my parents through— especially my mom. My schedule was packed with organized sports like soccer, baseball, track, golf, and tennis. In between I rode my single-gear bike everywhere. On any given day in the summer, I would ride 10 miles away to the Rock Point Bridge, where I'd leave my bike in the ditch on the side of the road and jump off the 60-foot bridge into the mighty Rogue River.

My best friend, Joe, and I used to climb to the top of the peaks surrounding Rogue River and play a game we called "no brakes" on the descent, which basically entailed running as fast as we could down the steep hills and jumping over any rocks in our path. I'm not sure how I managed to make it through my childhood without breaking any bones, but I certainly spent a lot of time with scraped-up limbs and skin that was swollen from poison oak.

One day when my parents were gone, I took a dare from my older brother, Rob, to ride my bike off the back of the bed of my dad's old rusty truck. I high centered on the tailgate and fell headfirst into the gravel, ripping up my face. I ended up needing stitches under my nose and in my mouth where the skin had ripped away from my jaw. My face was a massive scab for a few weeks, and I could only drink from a straw.

That didn't stop me from seeking out extreme adventures though. Whenever I saw a hill or even a big dirt pile, I felt some innate desire to conquer it. During my senior year in high school, I went camping with my parents in Mammoth, California. While everyone else was fishing, I decided to head out by myself with some cheap rope to scale the rocky peaks, like I'd seen people do on TV. I successfully climbed one and decided to rappel down, using the belt loops on my pants as my harness. Not such a good idea.

As soon as my body weight tightened the line, all six loops snapped loose, and I was fast roping down 30 feet without gloves—meaning there was nothing holding me to the rope except my two bare hands. As I strolled back into camp with bloody friction burns on both hands and all my belt loops flapping, my parents just shook their heads. After years of having me return from various adventures with cuts and bruises all over my body, it took a lot to surprise them.

•

Now, almost two decades later, I still had the same inner drive to push myself to extremes, but I'd matured along the way and gained a healthy respect for mountains. On top of that, I'd learned a lot about climbing techniques, safety protocol, and proper equipment. No more belt-loop adventures for me.

It's hard to trace exactly when my love for climbing began, but it may have been the ascent I made as a teenager to pour my grandma's ashes on the top of the mountain facing her house.

She and my grandpa lived across the creek from my family, so I spent a lot of time at their house when I was growing up. When I was 14 years old, Grandma was diagnosed with cancer and went through a series of aggressive chemo treatments. The treatments didn't help much; they just made her last few months miserable. One of the last times I saw her, she was sitting on the couch with a little head scarf covering her frail head. She waved me over to the couch, and I sat down beside her.

Pointing with her bony finger at the mountains outside the window, she leaned close to me. "Brian," she whispered, "I want you to sprinkle my ashes on top of that hill."

She was sure she was about to die, and even though I knew it was coming, I wasn't ready. My family was going to San Diego to see my brother graduate from Navy boot camp, and I was afraid she wouldn't be there when we returned.

I was right. After the funeral, my best friend, Joe, and I headed up the mountain with the box of her ashes. When I reached the top of the mountain, I made a cross out of some tree limbs, poured her ashes on the ground, and said a silent prayer. Then Joe and I ran down the mountain in our normal "no brakes" fashion, most likely in an attempt to make things as normal as possible and to avoid the awkward emotions that were rising up inside me.

I took my climbing to the next level when I ascended Mount Rainier for the first time in May 2008. A friend and I signed up with a climbing group, and I was both excited and nervous to explore at a higher elevation than I'd ever been to before. I was also eager to learn some technical knowledge about glacier travel. Leading up to the expedition, I trained on Mount Si, a smaller peak near my house, and when the time came for our adventure, I felt ready.

During the three-day expedition, our group learned various mountaineering skills, including rest steps, pressure breathing, rope travel, and self-arrest. I was surprised how strong the wind could be as we made our way to higher elevations, but it wasn't enough to stop us. It did slow us down, though, and it felt like for each step forward, I took one step back. I felt the rise of nausea in my throat, and my muscles were screaming, but I was confident I could do it. I put my chin down, placing one foot in front of the other, and suddenly we were there. We'd made it to the top! By the time I made it back to sea level, it was official. I was hooked.

After climbing Rainier several times, I summited other mountains in the Cascade Range, including Mount Shasta in California and Mount Baker in Washington. Mountain climbing tested my physical abilities and mental sharpness like nothing I'd ever attempted before. And even though I'd grown up surrounded by mountains, being on top of them gave me a newfound appreciation for their grandeur. There's just something about standing at the top of a mountain that's like no other feeling in the world. It's hard to describe, but a sense of complete calm comes over me as I try to take in the beauty and vastness of God's creation.

In the past decade of climbing, I've gotten one recurring question from people who don't climb: "Why do you do it?" The reasons for climbing are unique to each individual, and if you were to ask 20 different climbers the same question, you'd likely get 20 different answers. For me, it mostly comes down to the way God has wired me. I have a deep drive to set big goals for myself and then strive to achieve them. If I don't, I feel like I'm not living life to the fullest and becoming the person God created me to be.

I've also found that climbing provides a spiritual solitude that I haven't experienced anywhere else. There's something about being up there on the mountain heights that shows me the vastness of God in a way that's hard to comprehend when my feet are on level ground. While I respect the mountains, I truly respect and am humbled by the Creator of those mountains. As I've studied Scripture over the years, I've discovered that mountains are mentioned about 50 times in the Psalms, so I must not be the only one who thinks they give us a glimpse of God's majesty.

> You are glorious and more majestic
>   than the everlasting mountains.
> PSALM 76:4, NLT

Now that I'm a husband and a father, I get even more questions about why I climb. But honestly, I think that having a family makes me a better climber because it gives me an even greater sense of responsibility. That's not to say anything against climbers who don't have families, but I think that there's a unique kind of accountability that only mountaineers who are parents can understand. My faith and family always come first, so when I'm determining which peaks to summit and what climbing situations to put myself in, I always factor in my values. I pray about it and discuss it with JoAnna. Then, if I feel like God is leading me to go on a certain climb, I break my goal into achievable chunks to figure out what it would take to make it happen.

If I determine that the goal is selfish and would have a negative impact on my family, I scrap it. There are plenty of peaks around the world I'd love to climb, but I've abandoned them before I even got started. I knew that although they might have provided some sense of accomplishment and satisfaction, they would have taken away from family relationships and ultimately just fueled a compulsive drive to climb another mountain.

Here is my golden rule in climbing: I will never abandon my family. I had no idea how much that rule would be tested on the top of Everest on May 15, 2011.

•

Part of the reason I found myself on Everest that unforgettable day can be traced back to a simple conversation I'd had with a friend several years before. During a perfect summer night in 2007, my family and I were at the home of my close friend, Adam Henry. My kids, who were about the same ages as the Henry kids, were playing in the playroom upstairs, and our wives were at the table talking to each other.

Adam and I knew each other from work, and we'd already gone on some adventures together, such as rappelling, snowboarding, and mountain biking. But we'd never done any mountaineering before, so it felt completely out of the blue when Adam said to me, "We should do the seven summits!"

At the time, I hadn't even heard the term *seven summits*, and I didn't even recognize the names of most of the mountains he mentioned. I found out that in the climbing world, the seven summits refer to the highest peaks on each of the seven continents. Dick Bass was the first to climb all seven summits in 1985. He came up with the idea together with Frank Wells, who at one time had been the president of Walt Disney Company. But in the 20-some years since, only about 200 people had successfully completed the task, which made the challenge all the more compelling in my eyes. Plus, it combined a few of my favorite things into one dream: travel, audacious outdoor goals, and adventure.

I barely hesitated before responding. "Done!"

Of course, the reality wasn't as simple as my one-word answer that night. It wasn't something I wanted to decide flippantly.

When JoAnna and I talked about it, her initial response was, "Okay . . . but even Everest?" She shook her head, knowing that I was serious and that I'd probably already mapped out the whole trip in my mind. We talked about what it would mean for me and for our family, and we spent a lot of time praying about it and making sure it was the wise choice for us at this point in our lives.

Once JoAnna and I felt confident this was the right move,

Adam and I started making plans. However, Adam's quest was over before it began. One day while I was training on a local climb, he took his motorcycle out on a motocross track in Bremerton, Washington. He crashed after landing a jump, breaking his back in multiple places. He was helicoptered to Seattle's Harborview Medical Center, where several of his vertebrae had to be fused together. The doctors said he had a yearlong recovery ahead of him, so climbing at high altitude with a heavy pack was out of the question.

I continued to push ahead toward our goal alone, but I was grateful to still have his support and encouragement.

The first of the seven summits I attempted was Alaska's Mount McKinley, also known as Denali, or "the High One." I set out to tackle this 20,320-foot peak in 2009, but I had to turn back just shy of the summit due to high winds. The following year I climbed both Africa's highest peak, Kilimanjaro (19,341 feet), and the highest mountain in Europe, Mount Elbrus. Located at the southern tip of Russia, Elbrus measures at almost the same elevation as Kilimanjaro: 18,510 feet.

Next up would be the tallest of them all: Mount Everest.

•

Although I was already in good shape from the past few years of intense climbing, there were some extra preparations I'd need to do to make sure I was ready for Everest. Whenever I set a climbing goal, I tried to alter my training to conform to the specific conditions of the mountain I'd be climbing. For a mountain like Kilimanjaro, which has a high elevation but takes little technical skill, the best thing was to work on cardio since you can't really train for the elevation. For mountains like Denali and Everest, which are more than 20,000 feet, I added 60 pounds to my pack and did my best to climb three to four times a week. Sometimes I trained on Mount Rainier, which stands at 14,411 feet and is the most highly glaciated mountain in the lower 48 states. But most often I did my training on the various 4,000- to 5,000-foot peaks in my backyard in Seattle.

To emulate a heavy pack and to build up my climbing strength, I filled my pack with old laundry-detergent dispensers full of water. That way I could get a great muscle and cardio workout on the ascent and then dump the water at the top to save my knees during the descent. I tried to get on the trail by 5 a.m. to ensure that I didn't cut into work time or time with my family. I was usually back by 8 a.m. for my work meetings, with a Starbucks in hand for JoAnna.

On days I didn't climb, I ran six to eight miles on back-country trails near my house or swam across local lakes, such as Lake Sammamish or Rattlesnake Lake. I'm not a fan of stationary training (treadmills, pools, and stationary bikes), so if I have a choice, I'll always train outdoors. Not only does this regimen keep me in physical shape, it also keeps me mentally fit. You can never predict what will happen on top of a mountain, but it will never be as climate controlled as a gym.

Another thing I focused on during my training was making sure I had a solid nutrition plan. I knew I needed to make up for the extra calories burned in my workouts, but even so, that wasn't an excuse to indulge in unhealthy snacks (except my weekly box of Chips Ahoy! cookies). For ordinary training days, my diet looked something like this: I started the day with a bowl of oatmeal and a latte; lunch was a sandwich or a can of ravioli; and dinner was usually steak, pasta, or fish. For Everest training days, I still ate three meals a day, but I needed to fill in the gaps with constant snacks since I was burning calories almost as fast as I was taking them in.

The physical preparations for the climb were a lot easier for me than the mental and emotional preparations. Having been on several extended climbing trips in the past few years, I knew that the separation from my wife and kids would take its toll. And the past expeditions had been three weeks or less, which was considerably shorter than the two months required to climb Everest. But when you're heading to Everest, there are no shortcuts. Between the distance, the extensive traveling, the high altitude, and the long process of acclimatization, the trip couldn't be completed in less than two months.

I'm fortunate to have a wife who supports me in these endeavors. JoAnna and I discussed my trip plans often and in great detail so we felt like we were doing this as a team and remained unified in our vision. Many of JoAnna's friends told her they'd never let their husbands climb, and some of them even scared her with stories about climbing fatalities.

Unlike me, she is cautious by nature, but she is open to hearing my side of things. Before I went to Everest, I gave JoAnna an analysis of the various mountains I'd climbed to give her perspective. Mount Rainier has a history of 400 fatalities; Everest has only 200.[3] By those numbers, I'd already climbed the riskier mountain multiple times. Of course, she knew that there are lots of variables to consider and that many more climbers attempt the accessible peaks. So on a mountain like Rainier, the number of accidents increases based on volume alone.

But even though JoAnna has her fears, each time I leave on an expedition, she says, "Enjoy your time, but please come home safe!" It helps me to keep those words sealed in my mind so I can hold on to them when I'm stuck far from home at high altitude, surrounded by swirling winds and whiteout conditions.

Even with a supportive wife, though, there was no real way for me to prepare for being away, knowing that I would face real dangers in the months to come. But I tried my best to hide my sadness from my children. Although they knew that Daddy was climbing the highest peaks on the seven continents, they were too young to know the inherent dangers I would face. At ages seven and four, they still thought Daddy was Superman and could do anything. They were good motivation to make sure I was as prepared for this trip as I could possibly be.

Securing funds for an expedition can feel like an uphill climb in itself, especially for Everest, which is one of the most expensive climbs in the world. The Nepalese government requires climbing permits, which run $25,000 minimum for an individual climber. Then you have to pay for all the gear, travel to Kathmandu, and take a flight to Lukla, where the trek to base camp begins. And since climbing Everest requires an extensive team, there are also the funds needed to pay Sherpa porters, who help bring gear to base camp; climbing Sherpas, who provide assistance higher on the mountain; porters who carry and stage the equipment at higher camps; cooks for base camp and Camp II; and icefall doctors, who fix the ropes through the Khumbu Icefall. In addition, there are the incidental costs for things like food, oxygen, and tips.

I knew that Western-guided companies charge anywhere from $60,000 to more than $100,000, which was well beyond my budget. I chose to work with a Seattle-based company that had local connections in Nepal so it would be less expensive. I wasn't part of a large team, which meant I had Sherpa support and a climbing Sherpa, but for the most part I would be on my own. JoAnna was agreeable to this approach, but she insisted that I use supplemental oxygen. I agreed with her. In the 1920s, George Mallory and Andrew Irvine had helped remove the stigma that "real" mountaineers don't use oxygen, and now oxygen is used above 23,000 feet by more than 97 percent of climbers. There were some cuts I was willing to make for the sake of saving a few bucks, but oxygen wasn't one of them.

To help with the costs of the climb, I partnered with several sponsors. One was the AIDS Research Alliance, which raises funds with the goal of developing a cure for the epidemic. I'd be wearing gear with their logo on it to build awareness for them during my climb. I also connected with several product sponsors and a couple of financial sponsors. The rest came from out of our pockets—from the money JoAnna and I had been saving for this.

Beyond the physical, mental, and logistical preparations, I spent a lot of time focusing on the expedition itinerary. For me, the planning phase is what fuels my motivation and excitement. And since climbing is typically a team effort, I did my best to include my whole family in the planning process. It helped make things more real for me when I broke down each phase of the trip and shared it with JoAnna and the kids. It also helped to keep me focused. With all the potential distractions that threatened to keep me from accomplishing my goals, the planning kept me loyal to the reasons I was doing this in the first place.

I've found that focus is especially important in a sport like climbing, where there are so many vocal critics. One day when I was in the planning phase, I was at Starbucks with my family, and I was approached by someone who had heard I was preparing for an expedition to Everest.

"I heard you're climbing Everest," she told me. And then, right in front of my two young children, she said, "What are you thinking? You're going to die up there."

I paused and counted to 10, knowing I'd regret any gut-level response. I tried to calmly diffuse the situation and then turned to Emily and Jordan to see what damage had been done. Fortunately, with the white noise of various conversations and skinny vanilla lattes being frothed at high volume, they were oblivious to the verbal bomb that had just been dropped. It was one thing to prepare to scale a mountain that looms at the cruising altitude of a commercial jet. The line at Starbucks was something else altogether.

•

The final few months leading up to my Everest expedition were intense as I made sure the finances for the trip were covered, arranged to take unpaid time off work, took care of personal finances and bills, planned activities with the company sponsoring my trip, and maximized time with my family.

JoAnna and I wanted to be sensitive to how my trip would affect our children, and we were intentional about setting aside time to talk through everything together. With their different ages and personalities, we knew that Emily and Jordan would face this in unique ways. At four, Jordan had a hard time comprehending how long I would be gone or the vastness and risks of my climb.

One evening after dinner I sat down with Jordan and told

him a simplified version of my upcoming trip. When I was finished, I said, "Hey, buddy, do you want to ask me anything about it?"

"What kind of animals will you see there?"

Not many animals are tough enough to survive in Everest's harsh climate and high altitude, but I wasn't about to give my son something else to worry about. I told him about the few animals I knew could exist in the high parts of the Himalayas. "Well, there are a lot of yaks, which are like big, hairy cows," I said. "Anything else?"

"How tall is the mountain, Daddy?"

We looked out the window together, searching the skyline. "It's as tall as an airplane flies," I said.

"Is that as high as heaven?"

I smiled. "Not quite."

As a first grader, Emily was more aware of the dangers. She'd heard adults talk about the risks involved, and she had classmates who parroted back things their parents had said. And she was old enough to remember the last trip I'd gone on.

Emily was five when I'd gone on my first long expedition to Denali for three weeks. Three weeks seemed like an eternity then, but it was only a fraction of the time I'd be gone for the Everest trip. Denali stands at 20,320 feet, while Everest's elevation is 29,035 feet. Now, that difference may not sound like much, but in terms of altitude, those extra 9,000 feet are significant. The added elevation affects every aspect of the climb, from acclimatization to the duration of the trip to the gear that's required.

Emily has a strong will, and while I was gone, she had just continued on with her normal life. JoAnna told me Emily hadn't shown a ton of external emotion, which we knew meant she was internalizing her feelings. I understood her perhaps better than anyone else, because I tend to process emotions the same way. Knowing how hard the Denali trip had been for her, JoAnna and I wanted to be intentional about giving Emily space to talk through her feelings with us.

When we discussed things as a family, Emily tended to be quieter than Jordan, but when she and I had alone time, I made sure to ease her concerns. One day when she got home from school, I could tell something was bugging her.

"What's wrong, honey?" I asked.

"Nothing," she said. But she was talking in her little-girl voice, which meant there was something troubling her.

I kept probing, and finally the story tumbled out.

"Kayla's dad said you were going to die climbing," she said. She wouldn't look at me, but I could hear the quaver in her voice.

I wanted to give that dad a piece of my mind, but I knew that wouldn't change the way Emily felt.

"Nothing is going to happen to me, sweetie," I said. "I will be home with you before you know it."

When I tucked both kids into bed that night, I gave them the same reminder: "It's always harder before I actually leave," I said. "Someday you'll look back, and the trip will just seem like a blur." I said it to reassure the kids, but I was also reminding myself.

•

I was working for Cisco Systems, one of the largest technology solutions providers in the world. I liked it because of the people I worked with and the challenging work I got to do. Another perk was that my position allowed me to have a flexible schedule. I was able to work from home a few days a week, and they let me take chunks of time off for my climbs. In many ways it was a win-win, because I would also be testing and showcasing Cisco technologies during my trip. I had routers, wireless access points, 3G connectivity, tablets, and laptops spread all over my home office so I could get them ready to be used in a developing country, in areas where this type of technology had never been seen before.

My flexible schedule meant I was around more than most parents and could be present for my kids' school events and other activities. JoAnna and I made it a point to meet with Emily's and Jordan's teachers to talk about how my leaving might affect them in school.

Another way I got involved was through a program called WATCH D.O.G.S. (Dads of Great Students), which sprung up in schools across the country in response to the 1999 Columbine school shootings. This program encouraged dads (after they'd gone through background checks) to attend class with their children as an added layer of protection for the school. I got to hang out in Emily's class, help the teacher, eat lunch in the cafeteria, and play on the playground. I also had the opportunity to visit other classrooms to talk about my climbs.

One day just a few weeks before I was to leave for Everest, I was surprised when Emily's teacher, Mrs. Heinz, called me up to the front of the room.

"We have a small gift for you," she said.

Then she presented me with a handmade book. As soon as I opened the cover, my eyes started to fill with tears. Each student in Emily's first grade class had contributed a page with pictures and comments.

And that wasn't all. Looking a bit sheepish, Mrs. Heinz

pulled out something else. "It's a Snoqualmie Elementary School Cougar medal for you," she said. "For your trip."

I could barely choke out my thanks. These gifts and the students' support meant more to me than I could adequately thank them for.

As much as we were focused on how the kids would handle everything, I knew it wasn't going to be easy for JoAnna either. She had recently started a Christian counseling ministry at our church, Church on the Ridge. She was glad to have something to keep her busy throughout my trip, but it was going to be difficult for her to juggle everything on her own—the finances, the kids, her ministry responsibilities, and all the household tasks. But while she may not be a risk taker, she is tough, and she was up for the challenge. And she had known from the beginning what kind of person she was marrying.

We'd met 16 years earlier, when I was into extreme sports like snowboarding, rappelling, and surfing, and jumping out of helicopters in the Navy. I served in the US Navy for six years, and during that time I learned a lot of lessons that paved the way for my mountain climbing. I spent 18 months in training, including Air Rescue Swimmer (AIRR) school, which is widely considered to be one of the most grueling schools in the US military; Survival, Evasion, Resistance, and Escape (SERE), which provides training for land survival, interrogation, and prisoner of war (POW) tactics; and Helicopter Anti-Submarine Squadron training school. But the most significant lessons I learned revolved around staying calm and maintaining confidence in dangerous situations. That was certainly something that would come in handy in my upcoming expedition.

JoAnna and I couldn't have been more opposite, as she's deathly afraid of heights, but we understand each other and have come to respect the way each of us is wired.

And despite her fear of heights, JoAnna has made an effort to enter my world. She's gone on smaller local climbs with me, and she even joined me at base camp on Russia's Mount Elbrus. She loves the beauty of the mountains and appreciates why I do what I do. I imagine there are times she'd be happy if I were an average guy who worked from nine to five and sat on the couch on the weekends, but ultimately she knows I'd be miserable with a lifestyle like that and I'd be squelching the person I was made to be.

She fell in love with a guy who lived a significant portion of life with both feet off level ground, and she has a pretty good idea I'm not going to change anytime soon. It also gives her peace of mind to know that safety is my biggest concern, having seen me in action on trail hikes and climbs we've done together. She also knows that I'd give my life to save another, if the situation arose.

The one thing that kept both of us grounded as we prepared for this adventure was our faith. We prayed continually about my trip—for protection and safety for me, for the kids' adjustment, for JoAnna as she would be a single parent for a while, and for God to be honored through the trip.

During the church service the Sunday before I left, our pastor, Charlie, brought JoAnna and me onstage. All the church staff members laid their hands on us and prayed for a safe climb and a safe return. I hoped Charlie wouldn't ask me to say anything, because I didn't think I'd be able to open my mouth without falling apart.

•

And then one morning I sat up in bed, my heart pounding. The countdown was over. I would be leaving for Nepal in three days.

Everything had been checked off the to-do list—all except one thing.

I'd finished hiding two months' worth of gifts, notes, and surprises throughout the house to keep my family's spirits up and to help them feel connected to me. It was tough trying to find 60 different places to put each thing, so I put together a spreadsheet to track the locations, the gifts, and the clues. I then had my good friend Joe text a clue to JoAnna each day so she and the kids could have a daily scavenger hunt. Two of the gifts were prearranged trips—one to San Diego and one to Las Vegas. Not only would this give them something to take their minds off my absence, but it would also give them a break from the constant spring rain that hits western Washington every year. The kids' other gifts included things I knew they loved—coloring books, toys, and special notes.

There, I thought, when I'd finished hiding the final gift. *That should last them until I come home.*

Somewhere in the back of my mind, I heard that haunting question that I usually succeeded in silencing: *What if I don't come home?*

I felt confident I'd done everything I could possibly do to prepare. I was in excellent shape, and I'd mapped out everything for the next two months. But I also knew the reality: people do die on Everest. Things could happen that were out of my control—like severe weather, unexpected mountain conditions, or my body's response to performing at altitude.

I shuddered to think about the events of 1996. I was in the Navy at the time and hadn't started climbing yet, but the news still rocked me, as it did the entire nation. With 15 total deaths, it was Everest's deadliest year on record. During a summit attempt on May 10, eight people were caught in a blizzard and perished. While Everest isn't the most technical mountain to climb, there are many reasons it has earned its reputation for being the most dangerous. First of all, there are the geological hazards. Not long after base camp, you have to climb the Khumbu Icefall—basically a river of ice—multiple times. Along the route, you face the threat of avalanches, massive walls of glacial ice, and huge blocks of ice called seracs, which can be the size of buildings. Seracs are constantly moving, and they may topple with little warning.

Then you have to climb Lhotse Face—no easy task, since it's a straight-up ice climb for a few miles. Once you've made it up Lhotse Face, you enter the death zone (26,000 feet)— the altitude at which your body starts slowly deteriorating. Once you get above the South Col, or high camp, you face a fierce mix of rock, snow, ice, wind, and miles of exposed faces. Between the lack of oxygen and the high altitude, Everest boasts an element of danger that can be found on few other peaks in the world.

Another reason for the increased risk on Everest is that in recent years it has become easier for people who aren't fully qualified to attempt the climb, putting not only themselves but others at risk as well. As one of the poorest countries in the world, Nepal relies on the money brought into the country from travel and climbing tourism, which constitutes 8 percent of the gross national income. Some suggest that the requirements are too lax, allowing unqualified climbers to attempt major peaks.

But whatever the risk factors—some of which were under my control and others that weren't—I couldn't deny that a number of people had died in the very spot where I would be heading.

With that reality in mind, I did the one final thing I needed to do to prepare. I waited for my family to leave the house and then sat down at my desk.

If something went wrong on the mountain and I needed to say some final words to my family, I would have to plan for that possibility too. And since I probably wouldn't be able to say good-bye from the top of Everest, I'd have to say good-bye with the help of a video.

As soon as I clicked Record, I started bawling my eyes out. I tried to tell JoAnna and Emily and Jordan how much I loved them and my hopes for their future, but I'm pretty sure no coherent words came out the first time.

I tried again, attempting to keep my composure, but something about saying those words out loud and imagining my family hearing them undid me every time.

In the end, I just had to accept the tears.

"I love each of you so much," I choked out. "I'm so proud of you—all of you. Emily, I'm so sorry I won't be there to walk you down the aisle at your wedding. Jordan, I know you will grow up to be a good man, and I am proud that you'll carry on our family name. I think you know this, but I want to say it out loud: JoAnna, Emily, Jordan, you are my world."

I saved the video file and hid it on JoAnna's MacBook. Then I sent the hidden location along with an explanation to Joe, who was already handling the scavenger hunt clues.

I prayed that JoAnna would never see it.

CHAPTER 2

THE LONG ROAD TO NEPAL

Be still, and know that I am God; I will be exalted among the nations,
I will be exalted in the earth.

PSALM 46:10

SAYING GOOD-BYE to my family when I left for Everest was
the hardest thing I'd ever done. I wasn't going on a day trip
or a weeklong expedition this time; I'd be gone for two full
months. Not only that, but I was taking a leap of faith that
I'd be able to scale the highest peak in the world.

We kept things pretty low key and didn't have a big celebration before I left. I preferred to fly under the radar since
I was pretty much in my own zoned-out world and other
people aren't quite sure how to act in a situation like that.
Maybe it's a little like when a soldier leaves for combat in a
risky part of the world. What do you say to someone who
may not come back? You can act like everything is normal,
but it ends up being awkward no matter how hard you
try. I figured it would be better to have a party afterward,

celebrating a successful return, rather than having a bunch of hype prior to leaving.

My flight was scheduled for 1 a.m. on March 31. There's only a small window of time for Everest expeditions to begin since the climbing season only spans from April to early June each year. The summit stands at a 29,035-foot jet stream, which means it creates its own weather patterns. The monsoon season that occurs in late spring ushers in strong winds and a warmer air mass, making that two-and-a-half-month window the only relatively safe, predictable time to climb. And even within that time frame, there are only a couple of days that are suitable for summit attempts.

The day before my flight, JoAnna, Emily, Jordan, and I spent the day together at the Seattle Pacific Science Center, where they had a Star Wars display. The kids enjoyed checking out a replica Death Star and seeing the R2-D2 and Princess Leia characters walking around. Under other circumstances, I would have been pretty excited to see Boba Fett (the bounty hunter with cool weapons), but it was hard for JoAnna and me to take in the experience with the looming reminder of what lay ahead in the next 24 hours.

When we got home, we went through our normal nighttime routine, except that this time I put Emily and Jordan to bed without JoAnna.

After I tucked Emily in, I sat at the edge of her bed. She looked up at me with the shaky smile she gets when she's sad or upset.

I hugged her tight. "It's okay to be sad," I said.

At that, her tears started flowing. I didn't have any words for her, so I just sat there and held her for about 15 minutes. I tried not to let her see my face, because I had started crying too. And once I started, it was hard to stop. Before long, I was crying so hard I could barely breathe. *What am I thinking?* I asked myself. In that moment, I was inches away from backing out of the trip, if it would mean easing my little girl's hurt. But I wanted to be the kind of dad who followed through, the kind of man who did the things he'd prepared to do.

Finally I whispered a prayer for both of us and then said, "I love you so much, honey. Daddy will be home soon."

I walked out of her room, closed the door, and leaned against the wall. I could hear her crying through the closed door, and that's when I really lost it. I buried my head in my hands and sobbed.

After a few minutes I gained my composure and went in to say good-bye to Jordan.

I talked through my schedule with him again, reminding him what I'd be doing while I was gone.

"Don't worry, Jordy," I told him. "The time will go fast, and when I get home, I want you to tell me all the fun things you did while I was gone."

Jordan was acting so brave that it broke my heart. I hugged him tight and told him it was okay to cry if he wanted to. In an instant, his tough-guy facade broke. He held on to me, and as he buried his little head into my chest, I could feel the tears soaking through my shirt. When Jordan looked at me, he saw for the first time that Daddy cries too. We prayed together, and then I told him, "I love you more than you'll ever know. Now be brave—I have to go." I slowly closed his door.

Then I collapsed on the top of the stairs and silently bawled my eyes out. As difficult as those moments were, though, I was glad to make that emotional connection with my kids rather than having them hold everything in, only for it to come out later in some other form.

I knew it was time to move forward and get on with my expedition. Whatever physical pain lay ahead for me at Everest, I doubted it would hurt as much as this.

•

A friend came over to stay at the house with the kids while JoAnna and I drove the 40 minutes to Sea-Tac Airport. We were pretty quiet on the drive. What can you say in a moment like that? We'd been married for 10 years, and JoAnna really is my best friend. We didn't have to say anything to know what the other person was thinking.

My mind meandered back to the longest time we'd been apart. It was 1997, and we were dating at the time. I was on a six-month Navy deployment in the Western Pacific on the *USS Constellation*. But this trip was different—this would be my first extended trip as a husband and a father.

JoAnna knew what it was like to face tragedy and to stay strong in the face of loss. Her hero—her dad—was taken from her when she was only 20 years old. She was attending San Diego State University's psychology undergrad program when her father received a terrifying diagnosis: stage 4 glioblastoma. In nonmedical terms, that translated to a brain tumor. A malignant one. He passed away only a couple of months later.

This devastating loss created in JoAnna a fear of being abandoned or left behind by those she loved. She knew she couldn't go on living ruled by anxiety, so she set her mind on releasing her fears to God. Through the grief and sadness of this journey, she learned to lean on God in deeper ways than ever before. I knew she'd be strong through our temporary separation, but I still hated to say good-bye.

Thankfully, we lived in an era when technology made it possible to communicate with each other from the other side of the world. When Edmund Hillary summited Everest in 1953, the most he could have hoped for in terms of communicating with people back home was the postal service. But even at that, he probably would have made it home himself before his letter made it from Nepal to New Zealand.

We arrived at the airport early so I could pick up my satellite phone—my means of communication with my family for the next couple of months. There had been an issue with the delivery, so the company had shipped the phone directly to the airport. I arrived at the specified delivery terminal, waiting as airport personnel searched the arrival packages. Almost an hour passed, but there was still no phone. I asked the workers to go back and check in various locations. They came back empty handed.

I looked at my watch. Every detail of my agenda was planned out, and if I missed my flight, everything would be set back. I had no choice—I had to board the plane without a phone. I would try to get a phone in Nepal, but I wasn't sure how reliable the 3G network would be there. This was the first trip away that I wouldn't have continual contact with my family, and it was the longest trip of all.

JoAnna parked our SUV curbside at the departure terminal sidewalk. She wrapped me in her arms, and I wasn't sure I'd ever be able to walk away from her and go through the airport doors.

Finally I said, "I've got to go, honey."

"I know." She swallowed hard, and I could tell she was trying to be strong for me. "I love you. And Brian? Please be careful." The tears were streaming down her face by that point.

I gave her one final kiss and tried not to look back, dragging my two 50-pound expedition bags to the EVA Air counter. I glanced out the window and saw that JoAnna was still parked along the curb. Our eyes locked for a moment, and then I saw that the line was moving, so I knelt down to grab my bags and drag them forward. When I looked up again, I saw JoAnna running through the airport toward me. Ignoring all federal aviation rules, I left my luggage unattended and ran toward her, catching her in a dramatic embrace. It was better than a scene from a movie.

"Please hurry back," JoAnna said.

"I will," I choked out. "I promise."

I finally got checked in and made my way through security. At my gate, I met up with my friend Chris, who would be hiking to Everest base camp with me. At six feet tall, Chris is my height but with a larger build. He's one of the most positive people I know—the kind of guy you can grab coffee with and know for certain you'll have a good conversation, no matter the topic. I'd met Chris through work, and he'd gotten interested in the trek after hearing about my plan to climb Everest. He also had a personal connection with the trip since he'd lost a relative to AIDS in the 1980s and he knew I was partnering with the AIDS Research Alliance. Chris's plan was to participate in the two-week base camp trek, where he'd hike from Lukla to base camp, which is a 38-mile trip with more than 10,000 feet of elevation gain. It was nice to have the company as I traveled around the world.

After a quick layover in Taipei, we flew to Bangkok, spent more than an hour in customs, and then met up with Bill, who would be leading Chris and his group to Everest base camp and then climbing Everest independently with me. Bill had years of climbing experience as a guide on smaller peaks. He'd grown up in New York, where he used to climb in the White Mountains, and then the lure of the Cascades brought him to his current home in Washington. He told us that his goal was to climb Everest before he turned 40, which was just around the corner, and that his side goal was to lose some of his potbelly on the climb.

The three of us walked around Bangkok that evening, eating Thai food at a local mall and then hailing a tuk-tuk (an open-air three-wheeled cab) to get some supplies. That evening we went to bed early to combat the jet lag, but by 1 a.m. I was wide awake due to the time difference. Jet lag is a bit like acclimatizing to altitude: you can't force your body to recover quickly from either.

I used the time while I was awake to write my first blog entry of the trip. *Climbing* magazine had come up with the idea to follow my climb through occasional posts. I knew it might be hard to give updates depending on how reliable our connections were, but I was excited to have a way to document my journey for family, friends, and fans—a one-stop place for everyone to track my progress.

April 1, 2011

My Everest expedition has begun, and I survived saying good-bye to my family. It was the hardest thing I've ever had to do, but we got through it.

Earlier this evening I talked to JoAnna and Jordan on a Skype call from my hotel in Bangkok. It truly makes a difference to have real-time video interaction and be able to see the faces of the people I love.

It's hard to believe, but I leave for Nepal in a few hours. I'm ready—or at least as ready as I'll ever be.[1]

•

Although I was feeling healthy and mentally prepared for what lay ahead, there's always room for doubt. When I prepare for a major climb, it feels a little like getting ready for a final exam. You're confident you know the information, but you never quite feel 100 percent sure when you sit down to take the test.

I'd been training for this climb for years. I knew the route, I had the plan mapped out, and I was in the best shape of my life, yet the question lurked in my mind: *Am I really ready?* When you're up against a feat like climbing the highest peak in the world, I suppose it's healthy to have a little humility and doubt.

For our final leg of our travels, we took a Thai Airways plane to Kathmandu, Nepal. As we began our descent, I saw the Himalayan range come into view. The moment Everest became visible, everyone got out of their seats to catch a glimpse, and although people were speaking many different languages, the sentiment was the same: awe. It was mind boggling to think we were cruising at the same elevation as the summit, getting an eye-level view of the highest mountain in the world.

It was the first time I'd seen the peak with my own eyes, and the reality of what I was about to do set in. Even from an airplane, the mountain was an intimidating pyramid. It stood calm and unchanging, apparently beckoning anyone who had the courage to attempt to scale it. I was instantly humbled by its magnitude. *Will I really be able to stand on top in a month and a half?*

The plane circled the hills surrounding Kathmandu, which were dotted with shacks and rice paddy fields. After banking around several times, we landed in the Tribhuvan International Airport and stepped off the airplane into the hot, smoggy air. The interior of the airport looked like a high school gym. Luggage was piled in haphazard stacks, and customs officers were assisting people with no discernible sense of order. Chris, Bill, and I got our passports and visas stamped, and then we went to find our driver, who was scheduled to meet us at the airport. Along the way, we were inundated by locals who were offering their services to drive us or carry our luggage. Finally we met our Nepalese contact, Sagar, and carried our gear to his van.

Sagar drove the small van through Kathmandu, Nepal's capital city. The houses were stucco shacks stacked practically on top of one another, and the smell of exhaust was overwhelming. The streets and sidewalks were sprawling with stray cattle, chickens, and skeletal dogs. As we drove, I was overcome by the poverty some of the people lived in, with adults and children begging in the street. I couldn't help but think of my own children. What if they'd been born here, instead of in the security they enjoyed back home?

Sagar laid on the horn as he zipped through the chaotic streets. At one point during the drive, he turned around and gave each of us a local cell phone with a stack of scratch-off phone cards that we would use to recharge the SIM cards. Finally we made our way through a back alley to Hotel Yak & Yeti. Bill and I carried our gear upstairs to the room we were sharing. As I hefted my two 50-pound expedition duffel bags, I thought about the contents.

It had been hard to prepare for every situation while staying within the 50-pound limit. First, there was my climbing gear, which consisted of various layers to accommodate both the warmer, low-altitude areas and the ultrafreezing weather at higher elevations. I'd brought along a hard-shell GORE-TEX jacket, a light down jacket, and a full down suit, plus three types of gloves (thin trekking gloves, heavy guide gloves, and down expedition mitts), four pairs of socks, and a spare pair of underwear.

Then there was all my climbing gear, which took up a lot of space and didn't always fold up neatly. I brought along an ice axe, a climbing harness, a helmet, crampons, several carabiners, a jumar, a figure-eight, a knife, and various safety devices and ropes.

I had managed to cram in two sleeping bags—one for –20-degree weather and one for –40 degrees—an expedition backpack, goggles, and two pairs of sunglasses. On top of that, I had to fit in all my technological equipment: a camera with extra memory and batteries, a solar battery pack with solar panels, and a mini-laptop with 3G capabilities, which I'd preloaded with movies and pictures of my family. I also had lots of quick-energy foods: fruit snacks, Pop-Tarts, trail mix, freeze-dried fruit, mints, drink mixes, cookies, Reese's peanut butter cups, and a case of Snickers bars. And not least of all, I had the gifts for the orphanage.

I hoped I hadn't forgotten anything.

As soon as I got settled, I made a quick phone call to JoAnna. She answered with a high-pitched "Hi!"

I knew she'd been waiting anxiously for my call. Since I didn't have many minutes, we kept things brief. I filled her in on how my travels had gone and what we planned to do in Kathmandu. The kids were in school, so I asked her to pass on my love to them.

"Tell them I made it there safely, okay?" I said. "And remind them that their daddy misses them."

•

I rearranged the gear in my duffel bag so the Sherpa porters carrying it ahead to base camp would have the appropriate load. When getting your gear ready for an expedition, it's not just important to know what to pack; it's also critical to know how to pack it. If the weight in your bag leans to one side, it'll throw the carrier off balance or end up hurting his back after a while. The goal is to keep the bulk of the weight at the small of the back and then stack up the rest of the supplies evenly from there.

Once I made sure my first bag was evenly loaded, I focused my attention on my second duffel. This one would be carried by another porter, who would head with us to base camp, so I kept anything I'd need prior to base camp in that bag.

One of the important parts of a climb takes place during staging—before you even begin the climb. You don't want to carry high-altitude items with you for several weeks as you make your way to base camp, as that would mean expending a lot of energy unnecessarily. But you also don't want to wish you had certain gear that is now 30 miles and a week ahead of you.

Many people don't realize that climbing Everest isn't just about going straight up the mountain. It's more like a long cycle of climbing and then waiting while the body acclimatizes—and then climbing and waiting some more. If climbers ascend too rapidly, they experience the potentially life-threatening effects of altitude sickness.

During the periods of waiting, climbers stay at camps located at various elevations. The lowest camp is base camp, a rudimentary campsite at 17,598 feet. The next camp, Camp I, sits above the Khumbu Icefall at 19,700 feet. Camp II is situated at 21,300 feet, at the base of Lhotse Face, the fourth-highest mountain in the world. Camp III (23,700 feet) sits about halfway up Lhotse Face on what is basically a wall of glacial blue ice. Camp IV, or high camp (26,300 feet), is the highest camp in the world and is located in the death zone.

When we went down to the lobby of the hotel, we met up with the other trekkers who would accompany us to Everest base camp. Dawn was from Kentucky and had been to the Khumbu Valley on a previous trekking expedition. She was down to earth and full of good questions, wanting to ensure she got the most out of her experience. Carlos, a dessert chef from Texas, was born in Spain. He had a perpetual smile on his face, and he was always ready with a story about his family. Sam was in his 60s and from the Midwest. He had lots of previous climbing experience and quickly became the father figure for the group. Veronique lived in Quebec and primarily spoke French, but since her English was much better than our French, we stuck with English. She was in her mid-30s and was the only other one of the group who was also attempting Everest independent of a large climbing team.

That night we walked through Kathmandu to get pizza at the Fire and Ice Pizzeria. I took a deep breath of the night air, which was a dense mix of smog, dust, and gasoline. That certainly didn't feel like the right combination to be breathing prior to climbing Everest, and I wondered how it affected the people who lived there. The streets were bustling with cars and motorcycles as drivers laid on their horns and maneuvered into any potential gap they could squeeze into. When we crossed the street, it felt like we were playing a strategic game of Frogger, looking carefully in both directions and then running with all our might. I didn't know much about the rules of the road in Nepal, but I was pretty sure pedestrians didn't have the right-of-way.

After dinner I had to hurry to get back to the hotel to do a dry run with the video equipment for the next morning. Tomorrow would be a big day—but not because of anything related to climbing. I'd be going to an orphanage on the outskirts of Kathmandu.

In all my climbs so far, I'd arranged to visit local orphanages to distribute gifts and toys to the children there. For this trip I was working with the Cisco Systems philanthropic group to set up a live high-definition video call using Cisco equipment. The children at the orphanage would be connected to other children in various locations worldwide, and they'd all participate in a science project via live video. A scientist would be on the call, instructing the children on how to make musical instruments out of Popsicle sticks and rubber bands. We'd sent the Popsicle sticks and rubber band kits to the locations ahead of time, and I was eager to see the faces of the children, many of whom had never had their own toy before.

Back at Hotel Yak & Yeti, I connected my integrated services router, my wireless access point, and my tablet via Nepal's 3G network and successfully made a high-definition video call to San Jose. All was looking good for the next day.

In the morning Chris and I had a driver take us across town for the orphanage event. All the streets looked the same, and most of them had no signs at all, so I was grateful to have a driver. On the ride over, Chris and I talked through the plans for the event—at least the parts we could control. Due to electrical shortages in Kathmandu, the power was turned off in certain sections of the city for blocks of time throughout the day. These blackouts weren't scheduled ahead of time, so I didn't find out until that morning that this area of the city would be affected. But what else could I do? "I guess we'll have to plug and pray," I told Chris with a smile.

After getting lost a few times, we found the orphanage. Pushpa Basnet, who ran the Early Childhood Development Center, came out to greet us and give us a tour.

"In Nepal, when people go to jail, they bring their children with them," she told us. "There isn't a structured foster-care system available, so the kids end up behind prison walls for crimes they didn't commit."

The Early Childhood Development Center houses and educates the children until their parents get out of jail. They are taught life skills and are brought to visit their parents a few times a month. After seeing all that this organization was doing for these children, I wasn't surprised to learn that Pushpa had been named CNN's Hero of the Year in 2012.

As we walked across the main area of the gated community, the children, ranging from 3 to 16 years old, stared at us.

Out of respect for local customs, I took off my shoes when I went inside. I was led to an open room upstairs, where I was to set up my infrastructure for the event. I had a solar-charged battery pack, which provided power to my equipment, but the 3G towers were down, meaning I couldn't connect to the other locations. I was able to use my local cell phone to dial in to and talk to kids in Singapore, Hong Kong, and the United States—including JoAnna and the kids, who were in the Bellevue, Washington, office.

It wasn't ideal since the goal was to have the Nepalese children see the kids in the other countries, but they still seemed to enjoy it. I told the kids on the phone about my plan to climb Mount Everest, and then they were full of questions for me.

"What is the mountain like?" one boy from Singapore asked.

"What will you eat?" This question came from a girl in Washington.

"Where will you sleep?" another little girl asked.

And then came the question I got every time I talked to a group of children, no matter where they were in the world: "Where do you go to the bathroom?"

After the call, Chris and I went outside to meet the local kids and distribute the bag of toys I'd brought. I'd filled a single compression sack—a nylon bag with straps that compress the contents to conserve space. I crammed as many stuffed animals in there as I could, and the kids' eyes lit up when they saw what I'd brought. They lined up from shortest to tallest, and Pushpa made sure each child thanked me after receiving the gift. I left wishing I could have brought more.

•

We spent the rest of the day exploring the city. At one point we walked across a primitive cement bridge with a narrow river running beneath it. Immediately I noticed the strong stench of garbage fermenting in the humid air. I looked below the bridge and saw trash and waste scattered for miles in the water.

I turned to one of the local men who was giving us a tour of the city, trying to hold my breath. "Why is there so much garbage in the river?"

"Don't worry," he told me. "It will all get washed away during the monsoons."

"Washed away?" I responded. "To where?"

He gave me a blank stare and shrugged his shoulders. We kept walking.

Later that day we took a van up a steep, windy road to Swayambhunath, a Buddhist site at the top of a hill in the Kathmandu Valley. It is also called the Monkey Temple, after the "holy monkeys" that live on the grounds. Only about 11 percent of the Nepalese population practices Buddhism (most people identify themselves as Hindu), but almost every aspect of Nepalese culture is influenced by Buddhism. Swayambhunath is considered the most sacred Buddhist site in the Himalayas, and people from all over the world make pilgrimages there.

The van revved and sputtered in the heat, barely making it to the top of the hill. The complex had several stupas—dome-shaped shrines with prayer flags strung around them—and Buddhist prayer wheels at every corner. It wasn't long before I saw the "holy monkeys" the site was famous for.

"Don't make eye contact with them," the locals warned us. "The monkeys take it as a challenge."

Challenge accepted! I took a picture of a row of monkeys sitting on a ledge (which the people there called a monkey train). There was no response, but I was wearing sunglasses. I decided to test the theory by tipping my sunglasses down and winking at one of the monkeys. Before I even had a chance to put away my camera, the monkey was charging straight at me! Fortunately it stopped before I had to defend myself; otherwise I probably would have screamed like a girl and started swinging my camera. This was one story about my trip I knew Jordan would love to hear.

That evening we returned to Hotel Yak & Yeti to stage our gear and prepare for an early morning flight to Lukla. Our expedition was about to officially begin.

As excited as we were to get our journey started, we knew it was important to eat, especially since this would be one of our last real meals for the next two months. We went to the famous Rum Doodle restaurant, located in the Thamel district. This restaurant is famous for giving a free meal to those who summit Mount Everest, and even more significantly, for having climbers who have successfully summited sign their names on the wooden plaques that cover the walls.

As we waited for a table, I read through some of the names, dates, and messages people had left over the years. It was inspiring to see the list of those who had previously walked the difficult steps I was about to embark on myself.

On April 3 we woke up at 3:30 a.m. and got ready for our 5 a.m. flight to Lukla. Tenzing-Hillary Airport has the shortest runway in the world, which makes it one of the top 10 most dangerous airports in the world. If you don't take off or land the plane quickly enough, you crash into the mountain.

The Kathmandu airport was surprisingly busy for so early in the morning. As I looked around at my fellow travelers, I wondered what had brought them there. I figured that some were local Nepalese residents, some were doing one of the various treks in the Khumbu Valley or up to Everest base camp, and others were climbing smaller peaks like Ama Dablam or Lobuche. And a few were climbing the big one.

We were loaded down with expedition gear, and I was grateful for the assistance of our local Sherpa team. The Sherpa, a people group from the high slopes of the Himalayas in Nepal, are frequently employed as guides and porters for treks and climbs. They are known for their strength, endurance, climbing expertise, and ability to handle high altitudes.

Our climbing expedition had hired Sherpa porters, who carried our heavier gear to the villages ahead, as well as Sherpa trekking guides to lead the Everest base camp trekkers. When we arrived at base camp and Camp II, we would have specialized Sherpa cooks who would provide the food and then prepare it using portable gas stoves. Bill and I also had climbing Sherpas who would assist us for the actual ascent of Mount Everest. They would be there to guide us through the route and carry additional oxygen for higher camps.

The moment Pasang, one of our climbing Sherpas, entered the airport, I could tell immediately he wasn't just a local traveler or a casual climber. He was decked out in designer jeans, a light brown 1970s-style leather jacket, and aviator sunglasses. I took one look at him and said, "That's my kind of climbing Sherpa!"

Close behind him was Pumba, our trekking guide. Despite

his short stature, he was obviously strong. He told us he had a family in the lower regions of Nepal, and he'd have to be away from them for weeks at a time to lead climbing groups. But he was proud that this job enabled him to earn enough money to send his children to the university in Kathmandu.

Our Nepalese logistics folks proved their worth, as they managed to get us on the early flight. I breathed a sigh of relief as we received our tickets at the counter. I was glad I didn't have to wonder if we'd be sitting in the airport all day or if we'd have to come back the following day.

Bill and I rode out to the Yeti Airlines Twin Otter plane on a standing-only bus. To my surprise, we boarded based on weight—heavier people in the front, lighter people in back. As I headed to the back of the plane, I tried not to think too much about the delicate balance needed to get this craft off the ground with all the gear and personnel. The plane was pretty archaic looking, with pleather seats that folded down. The seat belts were frayed, and I wondered if they were there more for peace of mind than for actual safety purposes. I glanced out the window at the jagged mountains we'd be flying through and tightened my seat belt.

The flight attendant handed us a couple of cotton swabs for our ears and a piece of hard candy as the in-flight snack. I put the cotton in my pocket and pulled out a set of yellow foam earplugs from my bag. I closed my eyes, listening to the muffled sound of the engine turning over before the propellers finally growled to life. As the plane took off, we circled Kathmandu a few times to gain enough altitude to get over the mountains surrounding the city.

As we climbed higher, the Himalayan range came into view, but I had to look straight up out of my dirty, scratched window to see them. With their blue-gray color, the mountains blended into the sky, and it was almost impossible to tell where the rocky surface ended and atmosphere began. At one point we briefly saw the summit of Mount Everest peering through the range. A surge of fear and excitement coursed through my body. *This is really happening!* I thought.

I was so busy looking at the majestic view outside the window that it took me a while to notice that the pilot had put the plane on autopilot and was reading the newspaper. I guess he'd flown that route a few times, but even so, I would have appreciated a little more attention at the wheel. Almost as soon as the flight started, it was ending and we were preparing to land.

I looked out the window and saw a thin strip of runway about 1,500 feet long. There was a time it might have terrified me to see a runway built into the side of the mountain like that, but it didn't faze me as much after landing on numerous mountainous surfaces during Navy combat search-and-rescue training missions.

The pilot dropped the yoke and forced the tires to the ground. The engine revved as the plane came to a quick stop and then made a sharp turn to the right. My stomach flipped inside me, and in that moment I was grateful that the in-flight snack hadn't been more substantial.

Exhaling with relief, we stepped off the aircraft and made our way through Lukla to an open area across town to meet our Sherpa porters and trekking guides. At 9,383 feet above sea level, Lukla is the first town in the Khumbu area. It has a total population of about 200 people, most of whom are Sherpas. Pasang was a rock star in the community, having made three successful Everest summits in the past. His first climb had been in 2010 with Leif Whittaker, the son of Jim Whittaker (the first American to summit Everest in 1963). Pasang had summited again that year with Eric Larsen, a polar explorer, marking the first fall summit in many years.

I could tell early on that Pasang would be a good fit for our team. He had just turned 26 and was in amazing shape. Not only were his climbing skills excellent, but he was also really familiar with the mountains. And in terms of his personality, he was a great guy to have around—friendly, confident, and respectful, and he always cheered us up with a smile or a contagious laugh. We were in good hands.

•

Mount Everest is a mountain of many names. As Westerners, we know it best by the name given by the British in honor of Sir George Everest, the surveyor who charted much of India. Tibetans call it Chomolungma, which means "Goddess Mother of the World." The Nepalese refer to the mountain as Sagarmatha ("Goddess of the Sky").

Although the mountain has been revered for centuries, it wasn't until 1852 that it was officially declared the tallest point on the planet. The Great Trigonometric Survey of India, piloted by George Everest, measured Everest's elevation as 29,002 feet above sea level. But since Tibet's borders were closed, no one from outside the country was able to make summit attempts until 1921.

In 1924, George Mallory and Andrew Irvine set out to be the first climbers to get to the top. No one knows for sure what happened, but they didn't return to tell about it. They were last witnessed heading toward the summit before vanishing into the clouds, and they weren't seen again until

75 years later, when Mallory's body was found by a climber—largely preserved by the frozen climate. There were no photographs or evidence on him that indicated he'd reached the top. In all the climbs since, Irvine's body has yet to be found. It wasn't until some 30 years later, on May 29, 1953, that New Zealand beekeeper Sir Edmund Hillary and his Sherpa guide, Tenzing Norgay, became the first to reach the top of the world.

Now that I was in the Himalayas, about to meet Mount Everest face-to-face, I thought back to all the times people had asked me this question: "What does it take to climb Mount Everest?" Although there are so many mental and emotional components that go into enduring a climb like this one, people are usually wondering about the physical side. And they're right—doing such a significant climb isn't something you can pick up on a whim.

For one thing, the oxygen content at the summit is one-third of what it is at sea level. So if you were to take a bunch of people acclimated to sea level and place them at the top, their bodies wouldn't know how to respond, and they would pass out and die in a matter of minutes. As a result of research and years of experience, we now know that it is possible for people to climb high-altitude mountains. But it can't be done cold turkey—you have to follow the "climb high, sleep low" technique, which gives your body a chance to survive at higher altitudes. This process of climbing a few thousand feet and then descending to rest for a few days allows the body to produce more red blood cells. Since red blood cells carry oxygen to all parts of the body, the only way to survive at extreme heights is to condition your body to create enough to accommodate for the lack of oxygen in the air.

But this process takes time. At high altitudes, the body is starving for resources and goes into a hypoxic stage, meaning it's trying to survive with reduced oxygen. In this state, respiration depth increases, pressure in pulmonary arteries builds, and oxygen is released from hemoglobin to body tissues. That's the medical explanation, but in layman's terms, it feels like your body is gradually being overtaken by slowness and nausea. It takes about a month for your body to adjust enough to be able to attempt the summit.

From a psychological perspective, one of the hardest parts of climbing can be the waiting. With so much downtime during acclimatization, you have to be really patient and willing to listen to your body. Not only that, but it's also really important to pick the right climbing team, because you're going to be stuck waiting around with them for weeks on end at the various camps.

•

After gathering our gear, our group left for our five-mile trek into Phakding, a small village made up of a handful of huts, a few teahouses, and some local markets. The trail, which wove through a series of hills, was the same one used by local Sherpas and dzo—animals that are a cross between a yak and a cow. With the large bells hanging from their necks, I could hear the dzo coming long before I saw them. Since they weighed more than 500 pounds, I usually gave them the right-of-way.

The trail under my hiking boots was caked with dzo feces and droppings from the yaks we'd brought along to carry some of our gear, so I was constantly watching where I stepped. I also wore a buff around my nose and mouth to keep me from breathing in the particles in the air. Although the air was clean and fresh in the lower areas of the Khumbu Valley, the trail itself, with its dusty cow pies, was another story.

Along the way, I saw prayer wheels and Buddhist prayer flags that people had hung for good luck. One of the super-stitions common to the Sherpa is that the wheels have to be in constant motion, so I frequently saw people grabbing the wheels to keep them spinning.

I thought about my own Christian faith and how I felt a special connection with God in the mountains. As I watched people striving to make sure all the conditions were just right so their prayers would be heard, I was grateful that God hears us when we call out to him—not because we're good, but because he is good. "You will call on me and come and pray to me, and I will listen to you" (Jeremiah 29:12).

We hadn't hiked very far before we got to a metal suspen-sion bridge. I looked over the side of the rickety bridge and saw that we were hovering over a cliff that dropped more than 100 feet straight down to the river below. I knew this was only a small taste of what was to come.

For lunch we stopped at a village inn that belonged to Naga, one of our trekking Sherpas. The inn was basically a large open room for dining, plus a few places to sleep in the attic, which was accessible only by ladder. Naga's wife made us a big lunch of fried rice and potatoes, with an apple tart for dessert. All the food in the Khumbu Valley is fresh—not fresh as in recently purchased from the market, but fresh as in the vegetables are picked straight from the garden. And if you're having chicken for dinner, the family goes out and kills a live chicken, plucks the feathers, and puts it on the table.

When we'd been served so much delicious food that I couldn't take another bite, Naga's wife came back with seconds, smiling warmly at us with a few gold teeth. She had a child wrapped in a fabric sash hanging from her side, with another toddler running around at her feet. After lunch Naga and his wife presented Bill and me with white silk scarves as a way to wish us good luck on our journey. We strapped the scarves to the outside of our packs and carried them with us on our trip.

In Phakding we crossed another suspension bridge, which brought us to the other side of the village. We stayed at a teahouse there for the night. The scenery reminded me of Washington, with the evergreen forests, rippling rivers, and rocky cliffs. But when it was time to turn in for the night, I was reminded just how far from home I was. I thought about my kids and how I wished I could tuck them into bed. I couldn't let my thoughts linger there long, though—I still had a lot of nights to go.

The teahouse had an open area for eating and a small room that Bill and I shared. We had two beds and a bathroom with a toilet and a shower, which was a rare treat in the Khumbu Valley. The farther we went up the mountain, the fewer luxuries we'd have. Chances were, this would be the last real shower we'd have for some time.

We all met in the central dining area for dinner, where I ordered a pizza. It wasn't what you typically think of when you order a pie here in the United States—it was more of a hand-stretched, rubbery dough with some sauce I couldn't quite identify and a white cheese that definitely wasn't mozzarella—but it did the job. The most important thing to me was that it was fully cooked. Back home I tried to eat a pretty healthy diet, but here I planned to stick to a steady menu of pizza, potatoes, soup, and rice. I didn't want to risk falling ill from strange foods or unsanitary food handling. Sushi was definitely out of the question.

•

I got minimal sleep that night due to a lightning storm that lit up the sky for hours. The next morning the sun pierced a narrow laser beam through the window directly into my eyes, and it felt like a sniper was making a drop on me. Groggily I rose from my –20-degree Fahrenheit sleeping bag and packed my gear, shoving my down clothes into a small sack. It didn't matter how tired I was; I knew we didn't have time to spare. We had to keep pressing on to ensure that we reached our next scheduled destination on time.

Bill and I made our way into the eating area for breakfast, where we devoured a few flavorless pancakes and hard-boiled eggs. The day's destination was the village of Namche Bazaar, about six miles away.

After eating, I went outside, and as I applied sunblock, a young Sherpa boy came up to me.

"Would you open my bottle of Coke?" he asked.

As soon as I opened it, he grabbed his prized possession, shook it as hard as he could, and let it explode into his mouth. I smiled at him, wondering how old he was and what he did for fun. *Would he play LEGOs with Jordan if they lived near each other?* I wondered.

I felt guilty as I watched the Sherpas work, knowing my bag weighed more than 50 pounds on its own, and now they were putting another 50-pound expedition bag on top of it. With the total weight of 100 pounds, the Sherpas' forehead straps pulled back as they walked, exposing the whites of their eyeballs. It looked like the excessive force would cause their eyes to pop out of their sockets, but I couldn't argue. This was their system, and they'd been doing it this way for years. I could only say thank you.

We crossed a metal suspension bridge that hung hundreds of feet above a raging river. The sides of the bridge were adorned with colorful prayer flags flapping in the wind. On the other side of the bridge was the hill leading up to Namche Bazaar, which was nestled into the mountain at an elevation of 11,200 feet. The path was fiercely steep, switching back and forth for about a mile. I set out at my own pace, listening to music on my iPod and keeping a steady rhythm as I climbed.

The music kept me motivated, step-by-step, as I inched toward our destination. The words from Creed's song "Higher" resounded in my ears as I took in the scene around me:

Up high I feel like I'm alive for the very first time
Set up high I'm strong enough to take these dreams
And make them mine

At the top of the hill, I checked my watch. I'd made the climb in 30 minutes. I found a local store on the outskirts of town, where I paid 10 dollars for a Coke and a Mars bar. I climbed onto an overhanging rock and sat down, enjoying the cold soda and reading the book I'd brought along—Bear Grylls's *The Kid Who Climbed Everest*. The weather was perfect. The sun was shining and it was in the low 70s—warm enough not to need too many layers but with a cool enough breeze to make for a refreshing climb. I knew the days like this would be numbered on this climb, as the average May temperature on top of Everest is −13 degrees Fahrenheit.

It's those brief moments of bliss when I'm climbing that help me reflect on God's incredible creation. *Thank you for this amazing world you made, God. Thank you for a body that's able to do this and for the drive you've given me to make it happen.*

I looked out at the view and stood frozen in place, awed by the massive rock formations and the snow-covered cliffs that stretched as far as I could see. With the huge glaciers, jutting snow cornices, and ledges of snow that barely hung on over 1,000-foot drops, the scene looked like something off the pages of a calendar.

Behind me was the town of Namche Bazaar. With a population of about 1,700 locals, it was the largest town in the Khumbu region. The village had a variety of shops, several hotels, a bakery, a couple of monasteries, and a smattering of houses. At all times of the day, trekkers, climbers, and livestock passed through the main thoroughfare, which was little more than cobblestone and dirt. I didn't hear any sounds of traffic whizzing by or horns blaring, but there was the constant sound of clanging bells as herds of yaks stomped through the village. It didn't look much like Seattle, but to the Sherpas, it was a major city in the mountains.

After the rest of the group made it to the top, we headed to the center of the village to the teahouse where we'd spend two nights. All the teahouses and shops looked the same to me, so I was glad our Sherpa team knew where they were going.

Our teahouse had a large main area for dining, where we drank tea and got to know each other. We also had a chance to meet the other climbing and trekking groups that were staying there and would be camped near us at Everest base camp. We sat in the dining area at long, lacquered tables with picnic bench–style seating—playing cards, reading books, or just talking about the adventure we were embarking on.

Bill and I shared a simple room with two beds and a bathroom. The beds were just old mattresses set on the floor, and the bathroom had a toilet and a showerhead but no shower. There was a drain in the floor, so we had to spray ourselves with cold water and try not to flood the room as the water made its way down the small hole. It wasn't fancy, but compared to the kind of camping we'd be doing in below-zero temperatures soon, it might as well have been the Ritz-Carlton.

After a brief tour of the room, I realized that there were no power outlets. The teahouse owners knew what a precious commodity power is in the mountains, so they made a good business charging for a very dull charging station. I was glad to have my portable battery pack, which was recharged by the solar panels, so I didn't have to recharge there. I unraveled my solar panels in my room and attached them to the window facing the sun. As long as it stayed sunny, I'd have enough power for my phone, laptop, iPod, camera, and a small light for nighttime reading.

•

The following day we hiked up to an Everest lookout at 12,303 feet, near Syangboche Airport, one of the highest-elevation airports in the world. It was once used to bring in climbers for expeditions but was eventually deemed too dangerous. The shock to the body of being exposed to such a high altitude without time to adjust resulted in severe altitude sickness and even death in some cases. Most people can cope at elevations below 8,000 feet, but higher than that, the diminished oxygen can cause physiological issues. Each body has a different tolerance for altitude, but there's a point where everyone, even Sherpas, feel the effects.

The view from the lookout was perfect. There wasn't a cloud in the sky, and we took in the impressive lineup of peaks: Everest, Lhotse, Nuptse, and Ama Dablam. When we descended back to Namche Bazaar, some of the trekkers in our party weren't feeling well. A few of them had stomach issues, some were suffering with headaches, and others were simply exhausted. I'd had enough hiking experience to have a pretty good idea of how my body would respond—at least to elevations I'd made it to in the past. Typically I could go up to 12,000 feet without symptoms, but as I continued, I'd start noticing that my body wasn't 100 percent.

The next morning we set out for Tengboche, at 12,700 feet. Before getting on the trail, I went back to check the room to make sure I hadn't forgotten anything. When I got there, I noticed the toilet was sprayed with vomit. Bill hadn't mentioned anything to me, but apparently he wasn't doing well.

Later in the day, when we were hiking, I stepped in next to Bill.

"Hey, are you feeling okay?" I asked him.

He looked surprised. "Yeah, of course," he said quickly. "I'm fine."

Veronique was really sick, so she decided to stay in Namche for a few days before heading higher. She had hired two climbing Sherpas, and they would both stay with her.

They'd join up with the rest of us a few weeks later, at Everest base camp.

Initially the trail took us down about a thousand feet in elevation. It was nice walking downhill for a while, but I knew we'd be feeling it on the route back in a few months. Around 9:30 in the morning, we stopped for tea at a teahouse on the side of the main Everest highway. Some of the more adventurous climbers opted for yak butter tea, but I usually stuck with spice tea or milk tea—spice tea made with milk. I looked at my watch and calculated that it was 10 p.m. back in the States. I fired up my laptop and launched Skype, hoping to connect with JoAnna and the kids.

They were visiting our friends in San Diego—one of the surprise trips I'd left in the scavenger hunt—and I was thrilled to find that the kids were still awake. It was hard to take it all in: here I was with the Ama Dablam peak behind me, talking to my kids from the other side of the world. As I watched JoAnna and the kids through the screen, I thought about the symbolism of this mountain. It's known as "the Mother's Necklace" because of its long ridge sides, which look like the arms of a mother protecting her child. I swallowed the rock-sized lump in my throat, silently thanking God for the woman who was at home protecting our children right now.

I turned my computer around so I could introduce my family to our Sherpas, Pasang and Pumba, and the other members of our group. Pasang, always smiling and full of life, waved bashfully at JoAnna and the kids, his cheeks flushing red. Pumba introduced himself so quietly we almost couldn't hear him. I was proud to have my family meet the brave men undertaking this journey with me.

JoAnna, as always, owned the conversation.

"Where are you right now?" she asked. I knew she had our itinerary memorized, and she'd know if we were off track.

"How are you feeling? How's the team doing?"

I was glad to be able to tell her that I was feeling healthy and strong and that everything was off to a good start. The team had had a few bumps, but nothing major.

"I miss you so much," she said.

The kids crowded into the screen, talking over each other.

"Daddy, we got to go to the beach!" Jordan said.

"It's so warm here," Emily chimed in.

I pictured them swimming in the Pacific while I donned more layers and hiked into the cold heights of the Himalayas.

All too soon my battery was running low and it was time for the kids to go to bed. I was so glad to talk to my family, but as soon as I hung up, a wave of sadness overcame me. I wanted to cry, but the rest of the climbing team was in the dining area, lying on the benches and getting some rest. I didn't want to embarrass myself, so I just closed my eyes and took a deep breath. *Thank you for my family, God. Thank you that you're taking care of them even when I'm far away.*

After tea and lunch, we set out across an extension bridge that was stretched high over a raging river. But we had to slow down our pace when a traffic jam formed in the middle of the bridge. Our yaks had stopped on the four-foot-wide bridge and wouldn't budge. When a trekker attempted to continue across the bridge, one of the yaks charged him. The other animals refused to cross with their heavy loads. I'm certainly no yak whisperer, but they could have been resisting because they knew there was a two-mile hill with a 2,000-foot elevation gain on the other side.

The Sherpas tried pulling the yaks, whipping them, and even throwing rocks at them, but the animals were stubborn. They expressed their displeasure by kicking at anyone who came close to them. Finally, after much coaxing, the Sherpas bribed them across from the other side with food.

Once we got across the bridge, I took off ahead, letting the rest of the group know that I'd wait for them at the top. I listened to a mix of Casting Crowns songs while I hiked. As someone who lives in two very different worlds—the world of an extreme athlete and the world of someone with a strong faith in Christ—I've always loved the song "Here I Go Again." Climbing Everest was already giving me opportunities to conquer my fears and share what I believed, and I wanted to take advantage of those chances.

That old familiar fear is tearing at my words
What am I so afraid of?

The hill switched back and forth, with a couple of areas of off-trail climbing that required me to go straight up. I chose the most direct path and made it to the top of the hill in about 45 minutes. The top of the rise was a little more exposed to the elements since it was outside the tree line, making it windy and cooler, with occasional snow dustings. I found a flat rock to sit on and added an entry in my journal, which I wrote in daily.

I also reread the words JoAnna had written in my journal before I left:

You'd better come home, because you mean the world to me! I want to grow old with you and spend the rest of our lives together. Don't forget to read your Bible and pray—I know God will guide you just as he'll be guiding me here at home. He has a plan for your life, and I believe you will come home safely. Summit or not, please come home to us safely. Enjoy your time, cherish every beautiful moment, and we look forward to seeing you in nine weeks or less. I love you so much!

After about an hour, the rest of the trekking group arrived. We visited the Tengboche Monastery, one of the highest monasteries in the world. The monastery was originally built by Lama Gulu in 1916, but it has been rebuilt several times after being destroyed by earthquakes and fires over the years. We removed our hiking boots and entered through the small door. Once inside, I was met by the strong scent of incense. I watched monks dressed in burgundy robes lighting candles and chanting in Nepalese.

It started to snow lightly as we headed down from the monastery and toward a village called Deboche. On the final leg of our journey for the day, we made our way through a tunnel of pine trees and towering rhododendron shrubs. After walking beside me for a while, Pasang told me, "You are very strong. You will have no problem climbing Everest."

I found his comment to be reassuring, but I knew that being strong is only one piece of the puzzle. It's all about how your body does at high elevations, if you can avoid sickness and injury, and if the weather cooperates. So many variables are out of your control, and there are times you have to remind yourself of one of the cardinal rules of mountaineering: if things don't work out, the mountain will always be there tomorrow.

We stopped in Deboche for the night, and I noticed that the farther away we got from civilization, the smaller the rooms were getting and the fewer accommodations we had. I paid a few bucks to take a shower, and when I did, I realized that the little instant shampoo tablets I'd purchased were pretty much worthless. They turned into mushy paper, hardly producing a bubble, and I spent more time scraping the sludge from my hair than getting clean. At least the water was relatively hot, and it felt good to zone out under the light water pressure from the showerhead. The 10 minutes of hot water I paid for were over in a flash, and I grabbed my towel to dry off as quickly as I could. I put on clean underwear, but the rest of my clothes were the same ones I'd been wearing earlier. I alternated between a few pairs of socks, two pairs of underwear, a few shirts, and a couple of pairs of pants, which I would hand wash whenever we had a rest day and clear enough weather for them to dry out.

That night at the teahouse, I had my normal dinner of soup and pizza. I was relieved that all the villages seemed to have pizza as a dinner option. The cooks used dried yak dung for fuel over their fires, and I had no guarantee that they would wash their hands, but I'd do what I could to limit my chances of food poisoning. I ordered a Mars pie for dessert, which was basically a Mars bar cooked inside a breaded tart. It was no Chips Ahoy! chewy chocolate chip cookie, which is my vice of choice back home, but it was a nice way to end a successful day of trekking.

That evening we were all asked to keep quiet in the dining area because a group from the Dominican Republic was doing a live video feed for CNN. They were the first team from their country to summit Mount Everest, and the excitement in the air was palpable. I found out later that Karim Mella and Ivan Gomez were successful in their attempt and ended up being the first Dominicans to make it to the top of the world.

Later that night the group started talking about the most famous legend of the Himalayan region: the yeti.

"So what's the real story about the yeti?" one of the climbers asked the Sherpas in our group.

From the reading I'd done before my trip, I knew that Western explorers in the 19th century had returned home with tales about large, apelike beings. But the yeti has been part of Nepalese culture dating back many centuries before that.

As Sherpas from different regions offered descriptions of the yeti, I quickly realized that while the specifics of the legend vary from region to region, everyone had grown up surrounded by some kind of cultural lore about the abominable snowman.

"It's a wild man," one of the Sherpas said. "Like an ape."

"No, it's a cattle mixed with a bear," said another.

Another Sherpa painted a different picture: "It's a glacier being that hunts," he said. "It is very powerful, like a god."

As I lay in bed that night before our final trek to base camp, I wasn't afraid of the yeti. I wasn't afraid of the high altitude. I wasn't afraid of Mount Everest. I wasn't afraid of what this climb would demand of my body. I had only one fear: that something would prevent me from returning home to tuck my children into bed again.

As I drifted off to sleep, I took comfort in knowing that

while Everest might loom large and so might my fears, God was even bigger. Joshua 1:9 says, "Have I not commanded you? Be strong and courageous. Do not be afraid; do not be discouraged, for the LORD your God will be with you wherever you go."

Wherever you go. Even if it's 29,035 feet above sea level.

CHAPTER 3

VILLAGE HOPPING TO BASE CAMP

You make known to me the path of life;
you will fill me with joy in your presence,
with eternal pleasures at your right hand.

PSALM 16:11

ON THE MORNING of April 8, sunlight peered through the window as roosters crowed outside. I got up and packed my expedition bag and then went out to enjoy the sunshine.

It was my mom's birthday, and I wondered what she was doing 7,000 miles away in Kailua, Hawaii. She and my dad had moved there recently to take care of my grandmother, who had had a stroke. They were planning to stay in Hawaii for a while to make sure she was taken care of. Once she was settled, they'd move her into a nursing home on the island and return home to southern Oregon.

I set up my solar recharging battery pack to take advantage of an hour of sunlight before we left for the next village, Pheriche. As I unraveled my solar panels, a female trekker from another group bent over and let one go right in my direction. We both laughed, but I still stepped away in search of clear air.

Flatulence is one of the lesser-known hazards of high altitudes. High elevations cause increased pressure in the stomach, which in turn must be released. Among climbers, the condition is known as HAFE, for High Altitude Flatus Expulsion (a play off of HACE, or High Altitude Cerebral Edema).

The trip was already starting to get interesting.

The leg of the journey from Deboche (12,400 feet) to Pheriche (14,000 feet) wasn't very difficult, as it was just a long, gradual climb. The Sherpas wanted to make a stop along the way at a monastery in Pangboche to participate in a puja—a good luck ritual. As a Christian, I was committed to worshiping God alone and not bowing down to false idols, as the Bible talks about in 1 Corinthians 10. But I also knew that this was important to the Sherpas, and I respected their right to follow their own religion.

We dropped our packs outside, near four-foot piles of drying yak dung, and ducked through a low doorway to enter the monastery. According to tradition, a puja ceremony is performed before climbers attempt a summit. White silk scarves are tied around the climbers' necks, and a monk throws rice in their faces.

The ceremonial lama who was leading the puja, Lama Geshi, was battling a nasty head cold. He kept blowing his nose and coughing throughout the ceremony, and I was worried about catching a virus. I tried to take every precaution to avoid illness, but sometimes your immune system is breached by situations you can't avoid. I held my breath as much as I could, but at that altitude, I didn't last long before I had to come up for contaminated air.

When it was all over, I said a prayer, thanking God for being the one true God and asking him to keep our group healthy.

When we left the monastery, we were met with a lingering odor that smelled like a cross between a gun range and feces. The main source of fuel in the area was dung that people burned, so there were heaps of yak droppings left everywhere to dry out in the sun. And since the Sherpas used yak, dzo, and donkeys to carry supplies through the valley, the trails were littered with animal waste.

"If you breathe in too much dung, you get Khumbu cough," Naga told us. "You cough so much you break some ribs." Naga was one of our Sherpa trekking guides, and I had no doubt what he said was true. I put on the buff to cover my nose and mouth to prevent as much dust and decaying animal waste from entering my lungs as possible.

After a few hours of trekking, we reached Pheriche and unloaded our bags at the Himalayan Hotel, where we'd be staying for two days to help everyone acclimatize. Each room had two beds, and there was one bathroom on each floor. The bathrooms had no lights—a luxury I hope I never take for granted again. There was a shower available if I wanted to pay for it, but I figured I could last a few more days before my personal stench got the best of me.

The next day a couple of our group members were battling altitude sickness or stomach issues, so we mostly took it easy. But I was feeling strong, so I decided to climb higher to continue my acclimatization process. I was also hoping to get a phone signal on the hill since it had been a few days since I'd spoken to my family. Before I left, I'd told JoAnna not to worry if she didn't get a call from me every day since signals could be spotty. She told me later that every time her phone rang, she ran to it, hoping it was me, but it rarely was.

I went for a hike with Pasang up to about 15,000 feet, where we got a great view of Island Peak (20,305 feet). At the top of the hill I was able to get a cell signal, so I made a quick call to JoAnna. We knew we wouldn't have long to talk since we'd likely lose the signal soon, but it was worth the entire climb just to hear her voice. Her life was still in fast motion, and she had so much to fill me in on, while mine was the complete opposite. I knew it felt like a bit of a tease for her to hear my voice and then not be able to talk long, but we squeezed in as much as we could in a few minutes.

"Jordan has been acting out lately," JoAnna told me. "And both kids have been having nightmares since you left." For a moment, I wondered if they were having premonitions in their dreams, but I couldn't let myself dwell on that thought long.

While we were up on the hill, I was also able to take some photos for my sponsors with the Himalayan peaks in the background. I held up banners with their logos as Pasang took rapid-fire shots with my camera.

As we descended down the loose scree of rock, Pasang said, "You are a super strong climber. You and I will be standing on the top of Everest in a month."

I loved his confidence.

•

Back home I'd heard about famous climbers in publications like *Climbing* magazine and *Outside* magazine, but now that I was on an Everest expedition, I had the chance to meet some of them in person. A number of them were even staying in the same hotel I was in. One evening I talked to Willie Benegas, who holds multiple speed ascents on various peaks, and his brother, Damien, who were leading a group on the south side of Everest. They were attempting to be the first to summit all three peaks in one trip—Nuptse, Lhotse, and Everest. I later heard that Willie flew out of Everest base camp back to Kathmandu to get his eyes checked out.

Neal Beidleman passed through while we were there too. He's best known for his heroism during the 1996 tragedy, in which he stayed in the whiteout blizzard with his clients all night in the death zone. This would be his first time climbing Everest since the tragedy. I also met Mark Tucker, who had climbed Everest in the 1980s for a peace climb with representatives from Russia, China, and the United States. This time he was there as the base camp manager for Rainier Mountaineering, Inc. In base camp and Camp II, our group would be positioned next to the group led by Mark and Dave Hahn, who had summited Everest fourteen times—more than any other non-Sherpa climber.

The last night in Pheriche, I played a few games of hearts with Mark. Over the span of many expeditions, he'd spent considerable downtime sharpening his card-playing skills. He thought he had me figured out using deductive reasoning, but in the end I won the last round based on pure luck.

As we talked, we discovered that our plans for the trip were pretty much perfectly aligned. We were using the same Sherpa outfitter, Kili Sherpa, and we'd be attempting the same route.

After our last round of hearts, Mark stood up. "Well, it's time for me to turn in," he said.

I stayed up to listen to some local Nepalese music that

was playing on the boom box in the dining area and to enjoy the company of the true climbing heroes: the Sherpas. For decades their people had risked their lives to fix lines, carry supplies, and guide climbers to the top. No one forced them into their profession—they loved it, and many of them saw it as not only a job but also a passion.

I had great respect for them as individuals and as professionals, yet there was a sense of cultural inequality that made me uncomfortable. It didn't feel right that they would drop everything to help us and constantly call us "sir" or "ma'am." I certainly appreciated the help and the honor they gave us, but I would have rather interacted with them on equal terms.

I listened as the Sherpas told story after story about relatives who had died climbing Everest or other mountains. But none of them seemed deterred.

As a trekking Sherpa, Pumba didn't have as high of a risk as the Sherpas who went to higher altitudes, but he still had to be away from his family for long stretches.

"Why do you do it?" I asked him.

He shrugged. "Well, sir, I make money for my family," he said. "I want my son to go to university. I want him to get a good job one day."

I turned to Pasang. "What about you?"

"I always dreamed of standing on top of Chomolungma," he said. "Very high honor."

Then Pasang turned to me, changing the subject. "Are you feeling ready for tomorrow?"

I nodded my head. "As ready as I'll ever be."

Then it was time to head to my cold, dark dungeon for some rest.

The following day we woke up early and prepared to move

to Lobuche, a small village at an elevation of 16,000 feet. I'd been hoping for a hot shower, but the pipes were frozen, so I was out of luck—and probably would be for another couple of days. As we ate breakfast, I heard the distinctive sound of whipping blades. I looked out the window and saw that one of the members from another team had to be evacuated by helicopter because of some form of edema. It was a reality check about how quickly things can go wrong at this altitude and how important it is to recognize and respond to the warning signs before it's too late. It was also a reminder about how quickly some people are willing to bow out.

We left Pheriche and followed the meandering trail for a few miles through desolate, rocky terrain leading to some gradual hill climbs. At one point I looked over at Bill and saw that he was hunched over, standing off to the side of the trail. After losing his breakfast, he kept walking as if nothing had happened. We climbed to 15,000 feet and had tea at the base of what would be our most significant climb of the day. During the rest time, I found a nasty outhouse to relieve myself in that was only a slight improvement from the "facilities" I'd have as we reached higher elevations—little more than a bucket in a tent. Then I mixed some orange Tang into my water canister and took a few moments to sit and enjoy the view.

We continued up to the top of the hill, where the famous Everest Memorial is located. The memorial is made up of small stone monuments etched with the names of fallen climbers. It was another grim reminder of the reality that lay ahead. I didn't count the number of stacked rocks and chiseled memorials, but there were more than I liked to imagine. I walked by Scott Fischer's stone, recalling the 1996 tragedy.

He was one of the guides on that fateful night, and it was sobering to think that 15 years ago he had stood in this very spot. Seeing the memorial didn't instill fear in me, but it did give me an even stronger resolve to make sure I planned for all the situations that could arise. I wanted to be ready for any worst-case scenarios. As I'd learned in my military training, it's always better to overprepare—the goal is to make sure your training is more difficult than the actual task.

Shortly after the memorial, we approached Lobuche. As we got closer to the village, we saw a number of expedition tents at the base of Lobuche mountain, a common place for climbers to acclimatize before heading up Everest. Lobuche is very small, and when we arrived, I could see why. The weather was dry and cold, and it certainly wasn't the kind of place you'd see in a vacation brochure. The room Bill and I were staying in was tiny and freezing, so we spent most of our time in the dining area. The bathroom was an outhouse just outside our room.

After unloading my things in the room, I hiked up a small hill in my down booties, trying to see if I could get a phone signal to call home, but with no success. In the fading light, I looked out in the direction of Everest, although I couldn't see it from there. *We're only one village away from base camp!* I thought. After standing there soaking in that reality for a while, I noticed that it had started to snow, so I descended back to the village.

The next day we set out to tackle the last leg of our trip before base camp. The final village wedged between us and our new home for a month and a half was Gorak Shep, which means "Dead Ravens." Climbing from Lobuche to Gorak Shep wasn't too difficult in terms of actual climbing, but I knew we'd start feeling the elevation soon as we moved to 17,000 feet. But for now at least, I wasn't experiencing any altitude symptoms, so I continued at my own pace ahead of the group until I got into cell phone range. I stopped on the rocky cliffs and called JoAnna.

"Honey, it's so beautiful . . . really majestic," I said. "I wish I could describe it to you, but there aren't words to do it justice."

It was strange to think of her going about her typical day—taking the kids to school, going to work, doing the dishes—while I was spending entire days hiking from one Nepalese village to another.

"Where are you right now?" she asked me.

"Well, I'm standing at almost 17,000 feet, but I still have to look up to see the tops of the mountains. If I look to my right, there's a massive canyon where the Khumbu Glacier used to be."

"Is it really cold there?" JoAnna wanted to know.

"It's not too bad as long as I'm moving," I said. "But I think for the Sherpas it feels like spring. They've been walking for 30 miles in flip-flops and jeans. They don't seem fazed by any of this. They're climbing a mountain and carrying a hundred pounds in a basket strapped to their foreheads, all while talking on a cell phone!"

As I hung up with JoAnna, it started to snow. Behind me I heard the sound of clanging bells—the telltale sign that a herd of yaks was making its way up the trail.

•

When we arrived at the teahouse at Gorak Shep, I realized we had officially reached the point where it was nicer outside than in our indoor accommodations. At such a great distance from civilization, the resources were limited, and we knew we needed to adjust our expectations for room and board.

Many people were sniffling, coughing, and blowing their noses in the main dining area, so I sat with my buff covering my mouth and nose, only exposing my lips to drink an occasional sip of tea. Our frigid room was basically a prison cell, except that it didn't have the luxury of a toilet. Everyone shared a hole in the ground down the hallway. It smelled of sulfur, vomit, and other bodily functions, and I dry heaved into my buff as I forced my body to take care of business in the freezing temps. The ground was covered with fluids where people had missed their target, and the surface had frozen into a murky yellow skating rink. I wedged my down booties on each side of the wall, holding my breath and trying to keep my balance. The thought of slipping on the ice and crashing to the disgusting floor was more terrifying to me than the prospect of whatever dangers lay ahead on Everest.

That night at dinner, as I scanned the room of sick trekkers, I felt the beginnings of a cold in my nasal cavity. I ate my yak cheese pizza quickly and headed to my isolated room right after sunset. After posting a few photos to my blog, I bundled up and took some cold medicine to try to get ahead of any illness. Throughout the night, I was frequently awakened by the sounds of people vomiting, coughing, and stopping at the hole down the hall. I'd nod off, only to be awakened by the loud scraping noise of people unlocking and locking the old-fashioned padlocks on the doors. Even when I did manage to sleep, it wasn't necessarily a restful experience. Every time I fell into a deep sleep, my breathing went into autopilot, and the pressure from the high altitude took its toll.

When I woke up the next morning, I felt a chronic headache coming on. I tried to figure out what was wrong, but at high altitudes it can be difficult to self-diagnose. I might have been fighting the bug I'd been exposed to when I met with the lama a few days earlier, and my immune system may not have been working as efficiently due to the altitude. Or it might have been that my body was simply struggling to acclimate to the higher elevation. Most likely it was a mixture of both, but at that point the cause didn't really matter: the more significant issue at hand was that I was taking a turn for the worse. It had been more than a year since I'd had any type of sickness, and at that altitude, it felt like a ton of bricks was being pressed onto my head. But I wasn't about to miss out on the big day ahead of us. I took some medicine, drank a lot of water, and powered through.

Gorak Shep is the last village before Everest base camp. It's a common place for trekkers to stop so they can climb up Kala Patthar (18,200 feet), which gives the closest and most scenic views of Everest. Our group started out early and made our way up the mile-long trail to the summit of Kala Patthar. It had snowed a little bit the night before—just enough to cover the trail and make it slippery. This was the first time since we'd started the expedition that I felt the strain of the climb. With my constant headache, the lack of sleep the night before, and the high altitude, I knew I was going to have to be mentally strong to make it through the day. I kept a slow pace and took steady rest steps—a climbing technique where you pause between each step to rest and breathe.

As I made my way, step by intentional step, I thought

back to my days in Air Rescue Swimmer (AIRR) school. It was 1993, and I was stationed at the Naval Air Station in Pensacola, Florida. I'd heard that AIRR was one of the toughest schools in the US military, and now I was experiencing that reality firsthand. Our instructors tried to simulate every treacherous condition we might encounter one day. We needed to be prepared to jump out of a helicopter into the middle of the ocean to rescue a drowning person, or provide recovery and relief to people in various life-threatening situations.

In the middle of the four-week AIRR training, we were given the task of swimming underwater for 25 meters across the pool and sprinting back freestyle for 25 meters. Then we'd repeat the process over and over again. The goal was to sharpen our ability to control our breathing, remain calm, and avoid shallow-water blackout. It quickly became obvious that the candidates who surfaced frequently wouldn't make it through the program. For some of them, it wasn't so much an issue of what their bodies were capable of as what their minds could withstand. After a certain number of repetitions, they simply couldn't sustain the focus they needed to keep going, lap after lap. It was all part of the process of weeding out the physically and mentally weak.

As I focused on keeping my mind and body working together on the side of the mountain, it occurred to me that high-altitude climbing wasn't so different from AIRR training. Anyone can get into physical shape, but you have to be mentally tough to survive weeks and months in such harsh conditions.

At high altitudes, your body lets you know what's going on, and it's important to listen. In general, your systems tend to slow down at higher elevations. The higher you get, the more effort is required for each movement. It's common to experience nausea, dizziness, fatigue, and rapid heart rate, and when those symptoms set in, you need to focus on pressure breathing—taking slow, deep breaths in and then expelling air through forceful exhales. It's better to continue moving and take five-minute breaks every hour rather than breaking often, as doing so will kill your momentum and actually make you more tired. I moved forward, keeping steady with my breathing, climbing, and resting, just as I'd learned in training.

Thankfully, the weather was perfect that morning, and we made it to the top in time to embrace the blinding sunrise over the summit of Mount Everest. The wind was calm at the top, and I couldn't help thinking that it would have been a great day to make a summit bid. I had to be patient though—I still had a month to go!

We spent about an hour on the summit drinking tea from our canisters and taking photos. Climbers from another group were there taking pictures too, stepping out on the exposed rocks and smoking cigarettes. Back in the early days of mountaineering, cigarettes were considered one of the most essential tools for a trek. Climbers brought cases of cigarettes and lugged them up the mountain, believing smoking helped them breathe at high altitudes. Now we know better about the dangerous effects of smoking on the lungs, which need to be functioning at the highest possible capacity in oxygen-deprived areas.

We climbed up to the small pinnacle summit to take pictures. The surrounding peaks looked deceptively easy to climb, and I could see how they might entice even the most novice climber to stick around and explore. As I made my way down to the safer platform, I noticed a couple of European climbers wearing crampons, harnesses, and about 50 pounds of climbing gear. Without using ropes, they grabbed hand-holds and swung over the exposed rocky cliffs below. I made eye contact with Bill, and we both stared in disbelief. *Do they have a death wish?* I wondered. I considered saying some-thing, but I didn't cause a confrontation.

Here's the thing about a mountain: it won't set limits on you. You have to set the limits for yourself.

We descended back to Gorak Shep without finding out what happened to the European climbers. After eating break-fast at the teahouse, we went outside in the sunshine to pack our gear. I heard something on the roof and looked up to see a local Sherpa on the metal rooftop, sweeping excrement to the ground, which another worker had shoveled out of the small bathroom window. I moved my gear as far away from the projection area as possible, saying a silent prayer for health and protection as I did so.

And then finally, after weeks of travel and hiking from village to village, it was time to head to base camp. The route there was relatively flat for a couple of miles, with just 500 feet of gain. We had to weave around some large boulder areas that had fallen from high canyon walls. An icefall now hugged the right side of the wall, and the last mile of the trail was actually on top of the glacier. We took it nice and slow, since we'd already had our morning climb up Kala Patthar and there was no reason to exert additional energy.

As we hiked, our group spread out a bit. At one point I heard people yelling frantically about 200 yards in front of me. I looked up and immediately saw what the commotion was about. A massive rockfall had started on the hills above, and a bunch of boulders were toppling straight down in my direction. I ran ahead as quickly as I could, praying my legs would move faster than the avalanche. When it was finally safe, I looked back, my heart pounding. If I'd stayed on the path, it would have been all over.

I took several breaths to calm myself, shaken by the reminder that you never know when things are going to become unstable in the mountains. That rockfall could have started from the smallest of rocks getting dislodged and releasing bigger rocks, which then started a snowball effect. I thanked the people who had alerted me of the danger and whispered a prayer of thanks to God for protecting me, and then I continued to the edge of base camp.

Everest base camp stands at an elevation of 17,598 feet at the bottom of the Khumbu Glacier. The only way to get there is on foot. It's possible to pay a lot of money for a helicopter flight in, but people who do so face a significant risk of acute mountain sickness (AMS) due to the sudden change in altitude. Besides, the experience of trekking to base camp is amazing in itself, as it allows you to traverse through multiple climate zones, visit fascinating villages, cross massive suspension bridges, and see breathtaking terrain.

Our group's camp was on the opposite side of base camp, close to the Khumbu Icefall. This meant we'd have a longer trek on the way in, but we'd be closer when it was time to attack the mountain. The path leading into base camp is a rugged mix of rock, glaciated ice, mud, and yak dung. I'd always imagined base camp as something of a refuge—a place perched on a safe hill, away from the glacier. But in reality, camp is located directly on top of the glacier. As much as you prepare, there are always surprises—things you can't imagine until you arrive in person.

As I looked around base camp, I found it hard to tell who was there to climb the mountain and who was just part of a base camp trekking group. Most trekkers go in for the day and then head back down to other villages to avoid base camp fees, so I assumed the majority of the tents were for climbers and their Sherpa support groups who would be making summit attempts—either for Everest or for other surrounding peaks, like Lhotse or Nuptse.

I explored camp a bit before the rest of the group arrived and discovered that the camps were grouped according to climbing team or guiding company. There was also a medical tent in the middle of camp near the helicopter landing area. The Everest base camp medical clinic was established in 2003 during the 50-year anniversary celebration. I was grateful for its presence, but I hoped I'd never need to go there.

When the rest of the group arrived, we met our extended Sherpa crew, which consisted of porters, our base camp cooks, and our Camp II cooks. We also met Lakpa, our other climbing Sherpa, who would work with Pasang. Lakpa had gone ahead to help bring gear to base camp and establish our camping area. He led us to our communal dining tent, which was set up with a variety of hot drinks, snacks, and a propane heater.

As we took off our packs and got comfortable, our cooking Sherpas delivered a lunch of hot soup, something made of mushy bread that resembled grilled cheese, and sugar cookies for dessert. We enjoyed the moment, taking pictures, laughing, and reflecting on how much better life looked after getting food in our bellies and a little warmth in our fingers. We had an outdoor toilet and an outdoor shower, which were set up in tents propped over flat rocks. The toilet was essentially a bucket with rocks around it. You had to be careful not to sit on the frozen stones since they might rip off your skin in the cold. The shower had a solar-powered heating box that would provide about 15 minutes of warm water. Each of us had our own two-person tent with a foam mattress inside. Now that's what I call camping!

As a rule, the Sherpa are superstitious about taking showers the first day in a new camp. They're afraid that the combination of the climate change and the exposure to water will make you sick. But it had been days since I'd showered, so I decided to try out the shower anyway. There were some technical difficulties with the solar heater, so a few of the Sherpas on our team brought me buckets of hot water. I used a big cup to pour water out of the buckets and over my head and body. I was grateful for the warm water, and it felt nice to remove a few layers of filth, but I couldn't scrub enough to get any part of my body even remotely clean. And the longer I stood there in the cold, with my body and my immune system exposed, I wondered if there was something to the Sherpas' warnings after all.

Later that night I felt the wrath of a massive high-altitude head cold encase my brain. I was up all night coughing and blowing my nose, and I had a headache that surpassed anything I'd experienced before. Between the headache and the small tent, I felt claustrophobia setting in, and with the pressure from the high altitude, it felt like my brain was in a vice. I had a live sponsorship video feed at five o'clock the next morning, and I was worried I would oversleep and miss it. I got five-minute intervals of sleep and kept waking up to check my watch and make sure it wasn't 5 a.m. yet.

"Lord, please help me," I prayed. "Don't let these tent walls close in on me."

I pictured JoAnna and the kids back home, wondering what they were doing right then. As fever raged in my body and my hair matted with sweat, I imagined myself giving Emily and Jordan a hug. In that moment, I would have done anything to be transported back home with my family.

Finally morning came. I'd made it through the night. Although I was still weak and sick, I didn't want to miss my event, so I slowly made my way to the dining tent, where we'd be doing the video feed.

Since 3G coverage was spotty in base camp, I ended up having only EDGE coverage, which allowed me to dial in to the Cisco WebEx video feed. I spent the next few minutes talking with partners and customers of Presidio, the sponsor company. Mike French, the chief marketing officer, did a great job facilitating the event. That was a relief, since I felt like I'd been run over by a locomotive. Toward the end of the question-and-answer time, I was cut off when I lost audio connectivity from the local 3G tower, but by technology standards in a developing country, I counted the event as a success.

I stumbled back to my tent, drank some hot tea, and then quarantined myself for the rest of the day. It went from freezing during the night to about 80 degrees in the afternoon, so I forced myself to stay in the tent, drinking lots of fluids and sweating it out. Even though I'd read about the weather in the Himalayas before my trip, it still surprised me to experience the severe temperature fluctuations firsthand.

The weather on the mountain can change drastically within seconds, especially inside a tent that served as a sauna.

A cloud cover or a setting sun can drop the temperature by 20 degrees. On the flip side, if the sun is high overhead and reflecting off the blinding ice, it can get up to 80 degrees in a flash. While I lay in my tent, waiting for the fever to break, the Sherpa crew brought me food and drinks. *Well, it's not quite like being at home,* I thought. *But it is nice to have room service at 17,500 feet.*

In the early afternoon, everyone gathered outside the dining tent for another good luck ceremony before our climb. I was still feeling weak, so I tried to stay tucked away in my tent, but Pumba found me and asked me to join them. I stumbled out of my tent and found a spot to sit cross-legged. It wasn't long before I was shivering outside my sun-warmed tent. I was grateful that one of the Sherpas noticed I was cold and ran to retrieve my down jacket. The ceremony seemed to go on forever, and my head felt ultraheavy—practically impossible to hold up. I escaped back to my tent as soon as I could, hoping I wouldn't be missed.

There was only one person I wanted to talk to when I felt like this: JoAnna. I dialed her number and was relieved to hear it was ringing. We had service!

"How are you feeling?" she asked. I hadn't even had a chance to tell her what was happening, but she already sounded anxious.

"Not that great," I admitted, filling her in on the past couple of days.

"I saw the pictures you uploaded to your blog," she said. "Your forehead looked swollen."

"I'll be careful," I assured her. This wasn't something to take lightly, but I didn't want her to worry when there was nothing she could do.

After we hung up, I did a self-diagnosis and noticed some possible symptoms of high altitude cerebral edema (HACE), a condition that causes swelling in the brain, weakness, and headaches. If left untreated, you can fall into a coma and die. There is only one cure: to decrease altitude. I was already struggling with a horrible head cold, and I didn't want to wreak additional havoc on my body with the high altitude.

I decided I needed to get down to a lower elevation the following day in order to heal. Up to this point, I'd been strong and my morale had been great. This sickness had caused a shift in my mental game, though, and I knew I needed to get well as soon as possible.

Our group was planning to head down to a lower elevation for a few days and then climb Island Peak, so the timing couldn't have been better. I was eager to get moving to see if I would rally at a decreased elevation. This was something I'd never experienced before, so I didn't know what to expect. *Will I have to turn around?* I wondered. *Will I have to admit defeat before I even start?*

As I gathered my gear in preparation for the next day's descent, there was only one thing left to do—and only one who could help.

"Lord, please show me if I'm supposed to continue," I prayed in the silence of my tent. "If you want me to quit now, give me the wisdom to know it and the grace to accept it. And if I'm supposed to continue, then please heal my body and release me from this debilitating pain."

CHAPTER 4

INTO THICK AIR

Each one should test their own actions. Then they can take pride in themselves alone, without comparing themselves to someone else.

GALATIANS 6:4

THE NIGHT of April 13 was one of the longest, coldest, and most miserable nights of my life. I woke up often and felt the intense pressure of a pounding headache closing in. I lay there begging the sun to make its appearance, allowing me to depart my dungeon-like tent. In the morning I hastily packed and began my descent toward Dingboche, at 14,800 feet. At 17,000 feet I stopped at the teahouse in Gorak Shep and waited to have tea with the rest of the trekking team.

Everyone on the team except Sam and Dawn was heading down to make an attempt on Island Peak. Sam's goal was simply to trek to Everest base camp, which he'd succeeded in doing, so he would be heading home before the rest of the group. Dawn had bypassed Everest base camp for a few days to trek to the Gokyo Valley, and she was planning to reunite with the rest of the team in Dingboche to make an attempt on Island Peak.

As I rested in the dining room, I evaluated my body's systems. The 500-foot drop in elevation from Everest base camp to Gorak Shep hadn't resolved my problems—but then again, I hadn't expected it to. I knew I had a long day ahead of me before I'd be able to tell if the lower altitude would improve my condition. We all had tea together, and I said good-bye to Sam as he headed out in a different direction, toward Lukla. Then it was time for me to get moving again.

I took off toward Lobuche, where the group met for lunch at another teahouse. Because of the quick descent, I still wasn't feeling normal, but I knew I had to press on. The trail led me up a grassy ridge and over a mountain. As I focused on putting one step in front of the other, MercyMe's "All of Creation" rang through my headphones:

All of creation sing with me now
Lift up your voice and lay your burden down

I'd been carrying a heavy burden ever since I'd gotten sick. For the first time on this expedition, I'd been weighed down by not knowing whether I'd be able to do this or not. But as I looked at the creation around me, I was filled with un-expected peace. No matter what happened on the expedition, God was still God, and ultimately that was all that mattered.

I took off from Lobuche ahead of the rest of the group since my head was still being crushed at that altitude. I hoped I would find relief as the elevation decreased. With gravity on my side, I fell into a pleasant pace, taking in the vastness of the surrounding mountain range. It had been one thing to experience these picturesque sights with others, but there was something special about witnessing it all alone.

Despite my unstable physical condition, I was filled with a kind of joy I'd never experienced before—the kind of joy that made me want to spin around with my arms outstretched while singing, "The hills are alive with the sound of music!" But on the off chance that someone was watching me, I managed to maintain my professionalism.

On a hill outside the village, I called JoAnna, knowing that my cell reception might be spotty once I made my final descent. I wanted to get her take on whether I should continue and push toward a summit attempt, even though I already had a good idea of what she'd say. We'd talked about issues like this plenty of times in the past, and I'd always said that if there was a life-threatening situation and the choice was life or death, I would always choose life.

"What do you think?" I asked her.

"I prefer life!" she said.

As always, she was honest and encouraging. "It seems like you have two options," she told me. "If it's time to summit and you feel healthy enough, I support you in that decision. If you feel like it would be safer not to risk it, you can do this another time."

I tried to say something, but my words got stuck before they made their way out of my mouth.

After a pause, JoAnna said, "I'm okay with either option as long as the decision is made based on the better outcome."

I hung up the cheap local cell phone and stashed it in my pocket, trying not to let the tears fall. "Thank you, God, for the wife you gave me," I whispered.

I wasn't ready to check out—not by any means. But I

was weighing all options and taking an analytical approach. I wasn't going to back down from the chance of a lifetime if I didn't have to, but I also wasn't going to put myself in unnecessary jeopardy.

After our phone call, I got an e-mail from JoAnna:

> I want to encourage you to stay to climb if you are healthy enough to do so without any unneeded risks, because that's what you're there for. I know you are homesick and we miss you greatly, but you have to focus on your task at hand. This climb is a once-in-a-lifetime opportunity, and we will always be here waiting for you! Remember that I support whatever you decide. Your health comes first; if that's clear, then go for the summit. Even Emily said, "I want Daddy to come home, but I also want him to climb the mountain, because that's what he wanted to do." We are all supporting you!

The final descent into the village consisted of a series of dusty switchback trails. I finally reached Dingboche, where I could instantly tell a difference in the way my body felt. It was crazy to think that a place the altitude of Mount Rainier's summit (around 14,000 feet) now seemed like sea level. I could actually feel the difference in the thickness of the air as each breath pumped life into my body. It was almost like getting an IV filled with strength, energy, and motivation.

Naga was waiting in Dingboche with Dawn. They had successfully trekked to the Gokyo Valley, and now they were heading out to meet up with the rest of the group. Naga greeted me with a big hug and led me inside the teahouse.

The setup of this teahouse was a little different from others we'd stayed in. The rooms circled around the perimeter, with a common dining area in the center. In the middle of the dining room there was a wood-burning stove fueled by yak dung. One wall was covered with windows that offered a stunning view of Ama Dablam.

Naga could tell right away that I wasn't as strong as I usually was. "Are you sick?" he asked. "I know the perfect thing for you. Come with me."

He took me to the dining area, where he encouraged me to eat some garlic soup to combat my illness.

Sherpas swear by pure garlic soup as a way to stay healthy at high altitudes. *Well, what do I have to lose?* I thought. He'd been living this way for his whole life, and it seemed to be working.

I downed the entire bowl. My breath must have been downright awful, but with JoAnna on the other side of the world, it wasn't like I was going to be kissing anyone anytime soon.

As I waited for the rest of the group, I felt my frustration starting to grow. Did I really train for all these months, carrying 50 pounds of weight up and down local peaks during the early morning hours, just to be taken down by a head cold? I had prepared so hard for this moment and had taken every possible precaution, but here I was, nursing a swollen head. From a physiological standpoint, there was nothing I could do to combat the symptoms of HACE or chronic altitude headaches. At this point the only thing left to do was wait and think through my options.

I decided to stay an extra day in Dingboche while the rest of the group trekked ahead toward Island Peak base camp.

Even though I felt great compared to how I'd been doing at Everest base camp, I knew it was important to allow my body to rest rather than to jump right back to the altitude I'd struggled in the day before. I reminded myself that this was part of the challenge of climbing in the Himalayas—it's a mental game as well as a physical one. This wasn't like the peaks back home, where I could climb any of the Cascade peaks in a day if the weather permitted.

I had to be patient—something that didn't come naturally for me. But I was trying to make sure logic won out over my drive to push forward. If I did have some form of acute mountain sickness (AMS), I knew it could be fatal for me to risk heading out with the team. I'd been on climbs before with people who had AMS and wouldn't admit it, and it forced the entire group to turn around partway through the climb. I didn't want to be that guy.

I thought back to my days in Aircrew school, when we had to learn water and land survival skills. The instructors knew that in an emergency situation, if someone wasn't tough enough—mentally or physically—he or she would put the entire team in jeopardy. As a result, the training was intense.

We went through repeated training evolutions in aircraft crash and egress activities. The first one involved egressing from a helicopter that had rolled over underwater. For the second evolution, we wore full flight gear (including boots, a survival vest unit, and a helmet) and were tossed into the middle of a pool. The instructors hooked us up to an automatic pulley system and dragged us across the pool with a parachute that was attached to our harnesses. We had to right ourselves and then use quick-release mechanisms to get away from the hazard. For the third evolution, we were wrapped in a parachute and tossed into the water. We had to stay calm and just barely wave our fingers to create an air pocket that would separate us from the parachute and allow us to glide out. If we panicked, we would get more tangled, use up our oxygen, and drown. The task was basic survival: get untangled before you drown.

AIRR training, which followed directly on the heels of Aircrew training, was even more intense than the five weeks we'd just completed. The whole system was built around weeding out the weak or timid. The instructors wanted to identify those who would give up when conditions weren't favorable or when they got tired or scared, and then make sure they didn't graduate and become part of the fleet. Out there, it wasn't just your own life at risk but also your entire helicopter crew and the survivors in the water.

In the morning we'd work out in the sand, doing pull-ups, sit-ups, and push-ups "forever"—meaning we had to stay locked in the up position waiting for the instructor to yell, "Down!" Then we'd all go to the down position until he gave the command to go up again. Our arms grew weak and we wobbled frantically, but we didn't want to be the person to fall and let the group down. Eventually someone wouldn't be able to hold his or her weight any longer and would collapse face-first in the sand. Then the instructor would yell, "Zero, zero! Start over!" We'd do that for about an hour for each exercise until our muscles were like Jell-O. Then, after a five-mile run in the sand, we'd head down to the ocean or the pool, sweaty and covered with grit, to do intense conditioning swims.

I didn't know exactly how my body would respond to the high altitude, and I didn't want to let my teammates down. *Better to wait it out,* I told myself.

The next day I planned to climb five or six miles to Island Peak high camp at 18,200 feet with Pumba. I'd bypass base camp and meet up with the group for a summit push later that night. That would be a good test to see if my rest day in the thicker air was effective. If so, I could continue up to the summit for an acclimatization climb. And if I still wasn't feeling strong enough, I could always descend to lower elevations to get more rest. Either way, Bill and I would be heading back to Pheriche for a few days of rest before our ascension back to Everest base camp.

That night I settled in and wrote this blog entry:

April 14, 2011

In the end, I can only do what I can do. If after a week at lower altitude I'm still a risk to myself and others higher on the mountain, then I'll be ending my expedition early. I know God has a plan, and it may not be what I envisioned, but I'll trust his judgment and direction. Stay tuned . . .[1]

Sitting all day in my prison cell, also known as my room in the teahouse, was torture, especially knowing that the other members of the group were making progress toward their goals. After breakfast, I set up solar charger panels in the window of my room and lay on the bed, where I wrote in my journal, read a book, and listened to music, willing the hours to tick by so the next day would arrive and I could actually do something.

The worst part was that I didn't have a cell phone signal, so I couldn't talk to my family. I sat on my cot and looked through pictures of Emily and Jordan, wishing I were home wrestling with them on the living room floor. *What are they doing right now?* I wondered. *How are they coping with me being gone?* When I was climbing, I was distracted from the sadness of being separated, but that day I had too much time on my hands to think.

For about an hour, I stared out the window and watched a cow chew grass. Although at first this sight was a reminder of how trapped and bored I felt, her circular chewing motion was quite peaceful. It helped remind me that it was okay to take it easy and just *be* that day.

I thought back to my Navy days, when my group was designated for combat search and rescue (CSAR) missions. In addition to our primary overwater missions, we also trained to become aerial gunner qualified. We flew with night-vision goggles, worked with special forces, and prepped for overland missions. One of the places we conducted training missions was Kuwait, where we targeted the miles of destroyed tanks from the Gulf War for aerial gunner practice before flying into Camp Doha to refuel and get a warm meal. We also flew missions near the Iraqi border, heading out in the middle of the night with a cabin full of Navy SEALs or other special forces. We never knew what the full mission was; we only knew we were flying near enemy territory and were armed for war, if necessary.

But in between those adrenaline-pumping excursions, there was a lot of downtime where we just sat and waited for our next set of orders. We were on a constant emotional roller coaster, fluctuating between boredom and adrenaline, adrenaline and boredom. After a while, I became numb to fear and flew my missions with confidence, knowing that my training was all I needed to succeed.

There was no way I could have known at the time how that training would help me survive on the highest mountain in the world—going from moments of pulse-pounding intensity to long stretches of boredom in the span of a heartbeat.

•

The following morning I was up and ready to go by the time the roosters crowed. I packed my expedition bag, ate some porridge, and was on the trail with Pumba and my porter by 7:30 a.m.

With high peaks engulfing us, we wound our way down the trail toward the south side of Lhotse Shar. Since it was just the three of us, we were able to make good time. But even so, I was aware that there is continual risk in such areas. I really needed to understand my body and respond appropriately if something felt off, because the nearest doctor was miles away. And although Sherpas are well equipped for the mountaineering aspects of the journey, they aren't trained for medical emergencies, and the methods they use for treating injuries don't necessarily align with Western standards of medicine. In a worst-case scenario, I'd heard it was possible to call in an emergency helicopter to the tune of $5,000, but that was assuming there was phone coverage at that point. I needed to be on high alert at all times, aware of risks and staying attuned to my body's feedback.

After a few hours of hiking, we stopped in a small village called Chukhung for some spicy noodle soup and tea. While we sat at the table, two little boys stared at me from behind the door. Eventually one of them built up the courage to come up to me and touch my arm. I smiled at him, and once the other boy realized I was safe, he joined in the fun. Pretty soon both of them were reaching out to poke me. I thought about how strange I must look to them. Most trekkers stay on the main Everest highway to base camp and don't venture out to such remote villages, so they weren't used to seeing anyone who wasn't a Sherpa.

I guessed that the boys were just a little older than Jordan, and I tried to think of some way to communicate with them even though we didn't share a language. I found a magazine and folded a paper airplane for each of the boys. After a quick demonstration of how to toss it, they eagerly took the flight controls. As they played with their airplanes, I caught them casting shy smiles in my direction when they thought I wasn't looking.

Then it was time for Pumba, our porter, and me to set out on the trail again to meet the others on Island Peak. The trail was a gradual series of ups and downs on rocky ridges, and I was grateful that my body was feeling strong and responding well to the increasing altitude. Although I felt back to normal, I was still being cautious, having felt like death only 24 hours earlier.

To the left, we had a spectacular view of Lhotse Shar, and to the far right we could see Ama Dablam. I breathed in deeply, taking in the fresh mountain air. We made the five-and-a-half mile trek to the rest of the group in three-and-a-half hours. I heard a few excited shouts when they spotted me, and a few of them came over to slap me on the back or give me a hug. We were a team, and when one part of the team hurt, we all hurt. When one person celebrated a victory, all of us did.

Climbing the highest mountains in the world is a big commitment, not only in terms of expense, but also in terms of risk, time, and effort. Since this was the first time anyone from the group had been to Everest and the first time anyone except Bill and me had done glacier climbing and fixed-line travel, I wanted to do everything I could to ensure that they had a good climbing experience. Although Bill was the guide for the trip, I also was able to answer people's questions and give them tips when they asked for advice. I was grateful that my experience was being put to use for the benefit of others.

One afternoon the group was learning ice axe arrest (using an ice axe to stop a fall). As I was helping Carlos and Dawn, Dawn gave me one of the nicest compliments I've ever received. "It's reassuring to see someone who stays so positive, no matter what," she said. "I appreciate that you're always trying to help and always speaking so highly of your wife and kids."

The next skill on the agenda was jumar training. A jumar is a rope ascension device that attaches to your climbing harness. It has metal teeth that catch the rope as you inch up, ensuring that you never slip down the mountain. The ropes are set ahead of time by Sherpas and early climbing groups using periodic anchors—ice screws, webbing, or metal pickets that attach to rock or ice. Although Bill and I were the only ones with experience in using jumars, the rest of the team caught on quickly.

Each rope team consists of three to five people. I prefer to keep my rope teams at three or four, but five is still manageable. The team has to work together closely to manage the rope quickly and safely. A team of three can move efficiently and still be ready to pull off a rescue if someone punches through a hidden snow bridge into an awaiting crevasse. But a team larger than five starts to become unwieldy.

To provide the safest climbing conditions, the most experienced individuals are positioned at the ends, with the most skilled climber in front (also known as the sharp end of the rope). This allows the lead climber to be poised to find the proper route, set the anchors, and manage the team. The less experienced climbers are positioned in the middle of the rope and spread out by about 40 feet each, depending on how many people are on the team.

After the group had gotten down the basics of jumar training, it was time for a lunch of soup and sandwiches in a covered dining tent at base camp. Then we headed a mile up the rocky mountainside to high camp, which was situated at 18,200 feet. The trail switched back and forth up the steep terrain, but I felt strong—like my normal self again.

After setting up camp and preparing our gear for an early morning attack, we ate dinner—Spam sandwiches and fruit—then went to sleep. I slept soundly that night, grateful to be feeling healthy again. The next morning, however, I heard that many of the newer climbers hadn't slept much. They were either too sick or too anxious to be able to rest.

The Sherpa crew woke us at 2 a.m. with a delivery of hot tea, hard-boiled eggs, and biscuits. It was a beautiful night, with an almost-full moon surrounded by glittering stars, which seemed to glow brighter when reflected off the encompassing peaks. It was early, but that's the best time to start a climb on highly glaciated mountains. You want the ground to be cold and solid so the climbing gear will work properly. Later in the day, the sun turns some of the ice into slush and warms the glaciers, making them unstable. Plus, warming temperatures can result in avalanches kicking off and crevasses opening up.

After everyone packed their gear, Bill, two Sherpas, and I turned on our headlamps and led the way up two miles through the rocky terrain. Piercing winds sliced through my jacket as we slowly increased our elevation. There's something hauntingly beautiful about climbing at night. We had to focus on the placement of each step forward on the dimly lit path, and there was a cloak of isolation that fell over the group in the darkness.

As the sun peeked over the purple mountains, we reached a pinnacle structure, which required a great deal of effort to negotiate. A single slip would result in a 1,000-foot drop to the glaciers below, where you'd become a permanent fixture of the Himalayas. Chris hesitated on the other side of the obstacle but eventually made his way across to the platform. Once there, he sat down, his breaths choking into a sob. I sat down beside him and put my arm around his shoulder.

"It's okay," I told him with a small smile. "I won't tell anyone you cried."

He looked at me and let out a surprised laugh, which was exactly my intention.

Just above 19,500 feet we reached the Imja Tse glacier. We put our crampons on our feet, cached our poles, and switched to ice axes. Roped up in teams of four, we traversed major crevasses and seracs. At one point we got to a narrow passage that was impossible to get around. We'd have to go through it.

"It looks like we're going to need a fixed line for this," I called to Bill.

Fixed lines are ropes attached to the ice with ice screws or long metal bars called pickets. The safety line is connected from your harness to the fixed line using a locking carabiner.

This ensures that if you fall, you won't fall too far. (Unless, of course, the anchor doesn't hold, in which case you fall very far.)

We were now at 19,500 feet—more than 1,000 feet higher than the night before—and I was starting to feel the effects of the altitude. And we still had another 1,000 feet to go. Breathing the thin air feels a lot like swimming underwater for a distance, but in this case there's no fully oxygenated air to replenish your lungs. It feels like you're suffocating, and if you allow yourself to think about it too much, it's easy to have a panic attack and pass out. Fortunately my time as a rescue swimmer in the Navy had taught me to stay calm in oxygen-deprived, panic-inducing situations.

I couldn't help but smile to myself, even as I focused on putting one foot in front of the other. *There's no way I could have known 15 years ago that my experiences with the dreaded helo dunker would come in handy right now,* I thought.

As part of our training, we crashed into the water in a helicopter simulator, also known as a helo dunker, which is essentially a large canister that's suspended over a deep swimming pool. The instructors would load it with Aircrew, Marines, and pilots in full flight gear and then strap us all into our five-point harnesses. As the finishing touch, they'd blindfold us with blackened swim goggles. As the dunker dropped, the instructor would yell, "Brace for impact!" We'd slam into the water and flip upside down. Since a helicopter is top heavy, with its jet engines and propellers overhead, it typically rolls over once it hits the water. As it tips, the rotors break off and the helicopter turns upside down, sinking almost immediately. That's when it's best to safely egress the cabin.

Completely immersed, upside down, unable to see, oxygen deprived, and disoriented, we would wait for the commotion to stop and then calmly pull ourselves through the helicopter cabin along a designated route. We'd been given orders to exit in an organized fashion, careful not to kick the person behind us. It was common for some of the crew members to panic and bail out of an open door. Others would prematurely unbuckle their harnesses and get sucked through an open window.

I knew from my training days that it never helped to panic. As much as you might be tempted to flail and fight in the face of limited oxygen, the best thing for you and for the rest of the group is to remain calm.

We traversed a long snowfield to the head wall, which was 400 feet straight up, and then dismantled the rope team so we could individually attach to the fixed line. I tugged on the fixed-line rope and shook my head. *This flimsy thing looks like something you'd purchase at a hardware store to tie down a tarp,* I thought.

But we didn't have a choice—we had to trust this rope with our lives. But that wasn't the whole picture. I knew that ultimately I was entrusting my life into God's hands. *Lord, please keep this rope strong,* I prayed silently.

•

Island Peak is typically marketed as a trekking peak, meaning it's supposed to be a moderate climb. But it's by no means easy—especially at the time we were there. Our Sherpas told us that you can usually walk up the fixed lines with little effort. But at the time of our trip, the route was a sheer blanket of ice from top to bottom, so we had to rely on willpower, stamina, and upper-body strength.

We attached to the fixed lines, inching up with our jumars. It was an agonizingly slow process: gliding the ascender up to grab the rope, then front pointing our crampons into the ice, and finally lifting ourselves up a foot or two. We used the rest step method to ensure a gradual, consistent pace and slowly made our way up the peak. My pack, which was stuffed with additional layers of clothing I thought I might need, was weighing me down. So when I got to one of the transition locations, I ditched my down jacket, strapping it to a carabiner on an ice screw.

About halfway up the steep pitch, Carlos twisted his knee and decided he needed to head back. We asked if he needed help, but he was confident he could rappel down and make it to safe ground on his own. To my amazement, even when he was hurt, he didn't stop smiling and cracking jokes.

Bill and I continued our excruciating fall-and-die journey toward the top. I tried to keep a consistent pace, while Bill attempted rapid bursts with longer rests in between. Finally, we made it to the top of the fixed ropes.

From there, we just had the summit ridge ahead of us, which was a narrow, knife-edge cliff with more than a mile of exposure on either side. I dropped my pack, secured it to a picket, and clipped into the fixed lines. Bill was debating about whether he should go up with me or stay behind.

"How are you feeling?" I asked him. He didn't look like he was doing very well, and although it hadn't slowed him down, I knew that he was still vomiting after almost every meal.

"I'm feeling a little sluggish," he admitted. "But I want to go on."

We quickly climbed the remaining 300 feet to the top. I was pretty excited to be above 20,000 feet, especially considering I'd felt like death just two days prior. The summit was barely large enough for two people, so we briefly enjoyed the view, took some pictures, and then headed back down. As we were descending, we passed Dawn and saw her reach the top. It was her highest summit, and I was proud of her accomplishment. Chris made it to the top of the fixed lines, which was the high point for him. It's an incredible thing to witness people overcoming adversity—both external obstacles and obstacles within themselves—to accomplish something they'd only dreamed possible.

Our descent wasn't much easier than the ascent, since we had to rappel down the uneven surface of the ice wall. Some of the Sherpa crew tried tying the climbers off and lowering them down the face, but I didn't like the lack of control with that method. There were just too many risks involved—one false move could mean disaster. I decided to rappel down on my own, so I wrapped the rope around my figure-eight—a rappelling tool with two loops. The figure-eight locked onto a carabiner attached to my harness, which created friction against the rope, allowing me to descend rapidly while retaining some amount of control.

Bill and I waited for an hour on the Imja Tse glacier until the rest of the group made it down. We roped off in our original teams and navigated back to the pinnacle rock area, where we removed and stowed our crampons, harnesses, and ice axes in our packs. Once we were off the rope, we were able to move at our own pace, and I was glad to get moving. When I was halfway down the rocky trail, I saw Pumba waiting for us.

"Brian, congratulations on summit," he hollered. "May I carry your pack?"

Before he'd even finished asking, I was hurling my pack through the air toward his waiting arms.

"Absolutely!" I said. "Thank you, Pumba!"

I made it to high camp, took off my steaming boots, and collapsed on top of my −40-degree down sleeping bag. *There's nothing like the comfort of collapsing onto a puffy sleeping bag after a big climb,* I thought.

As I lay there, I tried to take in the significance of what I'd just accomplished. In climbing, you usually move on to the next thing so quickly that the moments of soaking it in are few and far between. They quickly become little more than blurred memories. Island Peak wasn't Everest, but it was no small feat. *Thank you, God,* I prayed silently, *for protecting me. For letting me be here right now. For this beautiful world you've made.* In no time, I'd drifted into a sleep so deep I might as well have been unconscious.

Suddenly I was awakened by severe spasms throughout my body. Although it startled me, these involuntary myoclonic twitches were something I'd experienced before, typically as REM kicks in. I hadn't been asleep long, but I felt rested and ready for the next leg of the journey.

Bill made his way down a little later, looking even more nauseous than he had before. After vomiting into one of the mesh pockets of our tent, he collapsed into his sleeping bag and fell asleep.

A little while later, our Sherpa cook came over with a tray of lunch items. I had a sandwich, fruit, and boxed juice, while Bill played it safe and just ate a few bites of an apple, which he wasn't able to keep down. After lunch I made my way around to congratulate the others on their successful climbs and descents. I especially wanted to check in on Carlos and make sure he was okay.

"How's your knee doing?" I asked.

"I'm ready to roll!" he replied with a grin. "Pumba will carry most of my gear, and I'll take it easy on the trek out."

It's a good thing Carlos was in high spirits, because we didn't have much wiggle room in the schedule. It was time to stuff our climbing gear into our packs in preparation for the remainder of our descent.

Bill and I led the rest of the group on the five-mile descent to Chukhung, where we'd stay one night before moving down to Pheriche. It was a big day of climbing, but we knew we had a lot of ground to cover. The trail was a gradual slope downward, which meant gravity didn't work much to our advantage. Not long after we set out, it started snowing pretty hard, covering the path as we made our way down.

I arrived in Chukhung before the rest of the group but waited in the falling snow to ensure that nobody accidentally passed the teahouse, since all the buildings looked so similar. Once everyone made it inside, we settled into the dining area for dinner.

It was the end of the expedition for the Everest base camp trekkers and the Island Peak trekkers. So while Bill and I would head up for the challenge of our lives, they would descend to Lukla and fly home in time to celebrate Easter with their families. Part of me envied their position, knowing they'd be home in less than a week, but I had no regrets. Sure, I wished I could hug my family, eat normal food, sleep on a comfortable bed, and enjoy the luxury of indoor plumbing, but I knew I was here to climb Mount Everest.

The trekkers ordered celebratory "Everest brand" beers, which exploded all over the table once the metal tabs popped due to the high elevation. Meanwhile, Bill and I stuck with our milk tea, and I ate my standard fare of soup and Himalayan pizza.

It was extremely cold in the teahouse, and the furnishings were primitive. The door locked with an ancient metal key, and the facilities consisted of nothing more than a squatter hole in the floor. I stumbled through the dark hallway and found the room where Bill and I were staying. As soon as I unrolled my sleeping bag, I got in bed and was asleep almost immediately.

The next morning I woke to see my windows frosted over from our breath. I dressed quickly and then went to the dining area to eat pancakes. After breakfast, Bill and I set off for a short hike down to Dingboche, where we said good-bye to Chris, Carlos, and Dawn. The Sherpa trekking team was joining them, but we'd meet up with the Sherpas again when they led another group into Everest base camp. We took a group picture, and then I hugged each team member. I was sad to see them go, but I was excited about what this meant: the next stop was Everest.

As I watched the group head out on their journey home, I felt a pang of homesickness. I'd been away from my family for two weeks, and I missed them more than I'd imagined possible.

I pulled out my journal and read the words Emily had written on one of the pages before I left:

Dad,

I will miss you so much and I love you too. Come home soon, please. You are so brave, and I want you to come home very, very soon. You are the best!

Love,
Emily

At four, Jordan couldn't write much, but he signed his name underneath Emily's.

As much as I missed my family, though, I knew I had to stay focused to keep up my momentum.

Bill and I headed over the pass to Pheriche. When I got to the top of the pass, I climbed a higher peak to see if I could get cell coverage to call JoAnna. I was desperate to give her an update, since the last she'd heard, I was having headaches and feeling miserable at base camp.

But when I reached the top, I was crushed to discover that my phone couldn't catch a signal. That meant it would be at least a few days until I'd have a chance to reach her.

Bill and I climbed down a slope of scree—a collection of small, loose rocks—into Pheriche and unpacked our gear in the Himalayan Hotel, where we would stay for two days before heading back to Everest base camp. After acclimatizing on Island Peak, we would be ready to go through the Khumbu Icefall to Camp I and possibly Camp II.

I wasn't counting out any physiological issues such as edema yet, but I'd felt strong all through my Island Peak ascent, and I was hopeful that my earlier issues were a result of a head cold rather than acute mountain sickness. I understood the need to spend a few days in Pheriche to replenish my body before ascending again, but the thought of having to wait any longer was enough to drive me mad.

When I'm climbing—or doing anything, for that matter—I like to be productive, to feel like I'm making forward progress. But I knew that this was a good opportunity to rest, pray, read, and record the highlights of my journey so far. It was also a good chance to discuss the climbing plan with Pasang and prepare for any circumstances we might encounter.

We talked through a lot of what-if scenarios: What if we bypassed Camp I and pushed to Camp II? What if we hit extreme weather? What if we joined up with another team to share loads and alternate the use of tents? This would allow us to cut the number of carries in half, as well as split the task of building the tents and setting up camp. The downside would be that we'd all have to fit in the same weather window and make sure we had access to supplies when we needed them.

And then there was the biggest question of all: What were our potential summit dates? We had a lot to do in the next few weeks to even consider a summit date, but it helped to work toward that end goal so we could build a solid plan—contingencies included.

The next day I decided it was time to do laundry. When your socks and pants aren't merely standing up on their own but also start running, you know it's time to take action. A hotel attendant delivered a couple of pans of warm water, and I washed and rinsed my clothes using individual Tide packets. The strong smell of the detergent burned my nostrils, but it was a welcome change in my musky dungeon. As I washed, the water instantly turned into a thick, muddy mess, and I had to change it out several times to ensure I wasn't transferring the filth and muck from one piece of clothing to the next. I didn't want to think of the dirt, dead skin, and yak feces particles that had made their home in my clothing. I'm pretty sure my laundry attempt wouldn't have met my standards for cleanliness back home, but at least my clothes were better than before. And the task kept me busy, distracting me from boredom for a while.

I rigged some climbing cord from one side of my room to the other to let everything hang dry. It looked like a giant spider had created its home in my room, and I had to use caution when entering to avoid getting clotheslined.

That afternoon I wrote in my journal, reflecting on all that had happened in the past couple of weeks. I had made it to Everest base camp, and I had climbed Island Peak— both larger-than-life goals. But the most important thing I'd done was overcome a major mental hurdle. Getting sick had knocked me down, but I'd been able to get up and keep fighting. I felt like myself again—physically and mentally strong, and ready to take on the world. I wasn't going to let a smackdown like that one take me out. I was ready for Everest!

CHAPTER 5

LIFE AT ALTITUDE

Trust in the LORD with all your heart and lean not on your own understanding;
in all your ways submit to him, and he will make your paths straight.

PROVERBS 3:5-6

ON APRIL 20, after two days of boredom and resting at 14,000 feet, I was eager to head back up to 17,500 feet. Bill and I left Pheriche after eating pancakes and hard-boiled eggs and made our way up the Khumbu Valley. I was focused on keeping a steady pace and moving forward, but at one point I looked back and saw that Bill was losing his breakfast. He kept moving, as if nothing had happened. I was concerned about him, but he was intent on continuing. I just hoped he'd either get better or throw in the towel before he put anyone at risk—himself or the rest of the group.

We spread out as we made our way on the six-mile trek, periodically meeting up for tea at the various villages along the way. I was in my own world as I took in the amazing views and listened to Switchfoot on my headphones.

We were meant to live for so much more. . . .
We want more than this world's got to offer.

A mile out of Lobuche, I checked my phone and was thrilled to see I had coverage. I made a quick call to JoAnna to bring her up to speed on the past week.

"Hi, honey!" she exclaimed.

I knew she'd been worried about me, but her voice didn't show it.

"Hey, sweetie," I said. "I'm heading back up to base camp. I knocked out Island Peak in a day, and I'm feeling back to my normal self. I'm ready to get started on this climb!"

"I'm glad you're okay," she said. "It sounds like you have your morale back." She paused, and I could tell that although she was happy for me, she had some mixed feelings. If I hadn't been doing better, there was a chance I would have been returning home early.

"I wish I could be there with you," I told her. "But I need to do this."

"I know." Her voice was almost a whisper, but I could hear the underlying strength in it.

I tried to push my emotions aside so I could continue on toward Gorak Shep.

When we arrived at the teahouse, Bill, Pasang, and I had some soup, and then I decided to complete the remaining two miles to Everest base camp while Pasang and Bill stayed an additional night in Gorak Shep. It made sense for Bill to remain at a lower elevation since he was still dealing with stomach concerns, but I didn't want to risk having the germs in the village wreak havoc on my immune system again.

As I gathered my pack and headed out alone on the

trackless route, large snowflakes started swirling in the sky.
Pasang radioed the base camp Sherpa team to let them know
that I'd be arriving later that afternoon. I bundled up with
a light down sweater and a GORE-TEX jacket to protect
against the elements. I moved efficiently, enjoying the solitude, and it wasn't long before I entered base camp. Our
Sherpa team greeted me when I arrived.

"You are a very fast climber," Lakpa said with a smile. At
just over five feet tall, Lakpa was a workhorse, making extra
carries to ensure that the necessary gear was set for the next
day's climbs. He had considerable climbing experience—
including five successful summits of Everest under his
belt—and he would be paired up with Bill for their summit
attempt. I was grateful to have him on the team.

I got my gear settled in my tent and then walked over to
the dining tent. I shook the newly fallen snow off the side-
walls and then unzipped the front flap. I was looking forward
to relaxing and warming up with some tea. I was glad to see
Veronique there, looking much better than she had a week
earlier at Namche Bazaar.

"Hey, Veronique! Welcome to base camp. How are you
feeling?"

"Much better," she said in her deep French accent. "I
stayed a couple of extra days in Namche, but now I feel
better." She gave me a thumbs-up.

After lunch I headed back to my tent. At base camp, your
tent is your home. My "home away from home" had two
extra-large expedition bags, solar panels, my iPod with a portable speaker, my −20-degree sleeping bag, and a mattress,
plus my snacks, clothing, and medical gear. Each item was
strategically placed so I always knew where everything was,

day or night. A pomegranate air freshener hung from the top of the tent in an attempt to mask my not-so-fresh stench. My weekly showers with baby wipe–baths in between weren't quite as effective as my hygiene regimen back home.

All through the day and night, I heard the thunderous roar of avalanches kicking off from the peaks surrounding base camp. Each one began with an awful cracking sound as an overhanging ice cornice broke loose and sent echoes through the valley. Once this force of nature launches, it's unstoppable. It hammers the entire area below, dumping clouds of snow on everything within hundreds of yards. After things settle, an eerie silence follows. The only evidence of the havoc on the mountain is a thin "waterfall" of loose snow that pours down until there's no loose snow left.

At night I was also awakened by the loud snaps and cracks of the glacier below as it shifted and broke apart. As awful as it sounded, though, I knew there was little risk of getting swallowed into the earth, since underneath the moving sea of ice was a solid bed of boulders.

Our camp certainly wasn't a spa resort, but it was nice to have a central station to call home so we didn't have to pack up and leave each day. On what amounted to a monthlong camping trip, I was glad to have one place that remained stationary.

In many ways, base camp was actually a step above my final week of SERE training, which was basically land-survival POW camp training. We spent the entire final week in the mountains and desert of Warner Springs in Southern California with no food, no sleeping bag, and no tent to protect us against the elements. The days were extremely hot, averaging above 100 degrees, but at night, the temperatures dropped to below freezing.

In preparation for the long, cold nights I stuffed a parachute with leaves and pine needles to make a makeshift sleeping bag. The instructors told us to spoon with our partners to utilize maximum body heat to survive the night, but I decided I'd rather take my chances with the pine needles.

For the first three days we lived off the land, with very few supplies. We made fires using the natural resources around us, built shelters out of brush, and ate plants and bugs. One day we caught a rabbit, broke its neck, skinned it, and boiled it to make stew to feed more than thirty ravenous SERE candidates. When I looked at things from that perspective, life on the mountain wasn't so rough. After all, I had a down sleeping bag and a cooking Sherpa who could do all sorts of magic with Spam.

•

Bill and Pasang made it to base camp the following day. That evening we staged our gear for an early morning climb through the icefall up to Camp I. When I woke up at 5 a.m. and exited my tent, Pasang was there waiting for me.

"Bill isn't feeling so great," he said. "He's going to stay in the tent and try to get well."

The news didn't surprise me. I knew Bill had been battling nausea for some time, and his cough was becoming a constant companion.

I ate breakfast alone in the dining tent and then geared up for my first climb above base camp. My stomach churned with nerves and excitement. *Today I'm going to breach the unknown,* I thought. It would be one of many milestones on Everest. As I laced my two-in-one insulated boots, I heard Pasang outside, chanting a blessing in preparation for our climb. I used the time to pray for us and for others on the mountain.

"Heavenly Father, please watch over Pasang and me during our climb," I whispered. "Please watch over the other climbers, and keep them safe too. Thank you for JoAnna and the kids and all my friends back home who have supported me through this. Give my family peace today, and reassure them of your presence. And please, Lord, let me return home safely to them."

I stepped through the flap of the dining tent to see Pasang hurling a final handful of rice at the puja idol. We checked our gear and ensured that our harnesses were double backed, with the webbing wrapped securely through the buckles. This was a critical step so the harness wouldn't accidentally unravel—an oversight that has resulted in a number of deaths over the years when people have slipped out of their harnesses and plummeted hundreds of feet below.

In the pale moonlight, I looked up the mountain and saw the flickering lights from other climbers moving across the icefall. It was time to make our way through the maze of tents to join them.

Pasang and I headed up the Khumbu Icefall at 6:15 a.m. with our crampons, harnesses, helmets, backpacks, water, and snacks. As we set foot on the two-mile stretch of ice, my mind was filled with stories I'd heard about building-sized blocks of ice falling and crushing climbers and about unforeseen avalanches taking out entire groups.

The icefall is the first obstacle you encounter when you come out of Everest base camp. It's essentially a series of massive ice blocks, called seracs, which can shift and fall at a moment's notice. This is arguably the most dangerous area of the mountain. Not only is it unstable, but you also have to traverse this gauntlet of death multiple times. Nepal employs a small group of Sherpas called icefall doctors to map out the route, fix the ropes, and anchor aluminum ladders across crevasses. The route can change daily as a result of seracs collapsing and avalanches kicking off from neighboring peaks. As we made our way through the icy terrain, I found myself extremely grateful for these icefall doctors.

For the first time on the whole trip, I was nervous—not so much because of the danger, but because of the unknown. I'd based so much of my mental preparation on what I'd experienced in the past, so it was challenging when I had no prior knowledge to build on and had to rely solely on my capabilities and the research I'd completed. In the climbs I'd done in the past, I'd made my way around plenty of seracs, but I'd never gone directly through one before.

Pasang and I moved efficiently toward our destination: Camp I, at 19,700 feet. Once I got over the magnitude of the undertaking, I was able to appreciate the otherworldly beauty of the icefall. With all the crevasses, ice formations, and frozen ponds, it seemed a little like being on another planet.

If it hadn't been for the high altitude and the ice, the climb wouldn't have been too challenging. But at that elevation, I had to work for every step. Thirty times, on 30 different ladders, we crossed deep crevasses and straight up-and-down seracs. Some of the chasms were narrow enough for single ladders; other places were so wide that two or three ladders had to be tied together and strung straight across the crevasse.

The ladders are simply lightweight aluminum ladders, battered and bent from being transported along the 38-mile trek and from years of abuse in the elements. They are carried up the mountain by porters, who lay them flat on the snow and then tie them together as needed to cross the crevasse. These ladders are then anchored on each side, along with safety ropes for climbers to clip into and hold on to while crossing.

When I stepped onto the first ladder, I had to decide what my strategy would be. Some climbers use the spikes on their crampons to latch onto the ladder rungs, while others teeter on the rungs with the middle of their feet. There are pros and cons to each method. Latching the crampon points is more stable, but there's also potential for the spikes to wedge in and get stuck to the rungs, making it difficult to step forward. The teetering method is risky because you aren't as stable, but if you have good balance, you'll be able to continue your forward movement and get across more quickly. I tried both methods and eventually decided that teetering was the better approach for me.

I was grateful once again that I didn't have a fear of heights. I saw the terror on some of my fellow climbers' faces and knew that each ladder crossing was sheer torture. They got on their hands and knees and crawled across, looking straight ahead the entire way. If they had looked down, they would have seen that a single misstep would send them plummeting down the 100-foot crevasse.

I felt strong as I climbed, and I was grateful my body was acclimatizing well. The route switched left and right to avoid major obstacles or potential hazards. The entire path was equipped with fixed lines, which the icefall doctors set out and adjusted daily depending on the changes in topography.

With the exception of just a few areas between Camps I and II, climbers are attached to fixed ropes at all times throughout the route. This ensures that everyone stays on the path, and it can help prevent injury in the case of a fall. The ropes are important as a safety precaution, especially when climbers are carrying loads and going to higher elevations, but they aren't meant to be used as a safety blanket for people attempting climbs they aren't prepared for.

The route seemed to go on forever. In past years, Camp I was lower, but due to the continuous downward movement of the Khumbu Icefall, it had been shifted to a higher elevation. I knew this would be beneficial later, when we were hammering our way toward the summit, but at that point I was starting to wonder if we'd ever make it to Camp I.

And then, at last, with practically no warning, we were there. Camp I is basically a cluster of 20 tents on each side of a large crevassed glacier. It's located at the bottom of the Western Cwm, also known as "the Valley of Silence." Cwm (pronounced *coom*) is a Welsh word that means "bowl-shaped valley," which is appropriate, since it's a gently sloping valley basin at the foot of Lhotse Face. The Western Cwm is two miles across, making it the largest crevassed section on the route—and the only place requiring five tied-together ladders to get across.

I didn't have any expectations of what this camp would look like, so I wasn't disappointed to see that it pretty much looked like any other camp I'd been to. If not for the elevation, we could have been on Denali, Elbrus, or Rainier. I looked out over the icefall toward base camp, but with all the steep-angled ice blocks, I could no longer see it. Looking the other direction, I saw a valley surrounded by four looming peaks: Lho La, Nuptse, Lhotse, and of course, Everest, towering over the world.

It was extremely cold and windy up at Camp I, but I barely noticed. I was so excited to be this much closer to my goal. The summit of Everest is visible from only a few locations throughout the Khumbu Valley, but from where I stood in that moment, I had a clear view. After so many years of reading books, hearing stories, and watching movies about Everest, I was finally here, in the shadow of the real thing. It felt surreal—the mountain was right there, yet it still seemed a universe away.

I saw other climbing teams and Sherpa porters heading up the great valley to Camp II, and I wished I could join them. But I knew my time would come. For now I needed to listen to my body and be patient.

•

Hoping to get relief from the wind, Pasang and I rested for a few minutes behind a tent, where we ate a quick lunch of bread, hard-boiled eggs, cheese, fruit, and juice boxes. It was the best meal I'd had in a long time. After lunch we decided to head back down to base camp before the sun heated up the path and made things unstable. Despite the assistance of gravity, going downhill wasn't that easy, since we still had to negotiate our way through the ever-changing icefall. One area had seracs the size of a two-story house leaning against each other. As we made our way between them, it felt like we were walking down a very narrow hallway—a cold one, at that. I knew the formation wouldn't stay in place much longer, so I tightened my helmet and hurried through the tunnel to avoid getting crushed.

The next challenge Pasang and I faced was rappelling over an ice cliff with ropes anchored to a pair of aluminum pickets. I made sure to double-check the anchors, locking the carabiners and webbing and checking for any weak or frayed areas. It wasn't ideal, but with two anchors, I felt confident that even if one broke, the other would catch.

Back home, I led Extreme Adventures rappelling events for my church, but that was much easier since I didn't have all the gear that was required on Everest. At our church events, I wore shorts and light hiking boots, and I didn't have a 50-pound pack on my back.

My crampons stuck to the ice, slowing my momentum, and the rope slipped back and forth on the ice-pivot area. Finally I was able to make my way down safely. After crossing several more ladders, this process started to become more comfortable for me, but I knew I needed to guard against becoming complacent. After a long day, it's easy to get sloppy and make mistakes—in fact, most accidents occur on the way down.

And even when you're on high alert, things can still go wrong. Just as I was making my way across a crevasse where three ladders were tied together, I experienced one of a climber's worst nightmares.

As I carefully placed my crampons on each rung, I kept a firm grasp on a single fixed rope. Then, when I was in the middle of the ladder, the rope suddenly came free of its anchor. I lost my balance but tried to stay calm, kneeling down to lower my center of gravity. I grabbed hold of the rungs with both hands and then carefully inched my way across without a safety line.

"Thank you, God," I breathed as I reached the other side.

I'd heard stories of climbers who had fallen into crevasses below, and their bodies weren't found until years later, when they were churned out by the glacier miles from base camp. And during my 2009 Denali expedition, one of our team members in the middle of the rope tripped on some bullet-proof glacial ice. He fell straight on his ice axe and ended up breaking several ribs.

I was determined to keep focused on each step. I knew I wouldn't be safe until I was back in my tent.

I'd learned a lot about the importance of focus during my Navy days. In the second week of AIRR training, we were put through an extensive lifesaving course, where we learned techniques to gain control of active survivors in emergency situations. The first thing we had to do was force the survivor deep underwater, which usually causes panicked survivors to panic more and release control, making it easier for the rescuer to get the upper hand after they surface. But since this was AIRR training, we were learning worst-case scenarios, which meant the instructors who were role-playing the survivors never released control. We dove deep with the latched-on survivor and then applied various pressure points to turn the victim's back toward us. That would enable us to lock control with a cross-chest carry.

A lot of candidates were weeded out during this portion of the training. They simply weren't able to stay calm underwater for long periods of time. In one particularly intense training session, I was attacked from behind by a survivor. I brought him deep underwater until he was in a state of panic, and then I turned him around and gained control at the surface. But I'd missed one pressure point—a specific spot near his elbow.

The instructor, who was underwater evaluating me, took me to the side of the pool and let me know where I'd gone wrong. "Airman Dickinson, you failed the rear head hold release procedure," he barked. "You have one more chance to pass, or you're gone!"

I nodded, closed my eyes, and pushed off the side of the pool to tread water. In a split second, I was hit by a force that felt like a refrigerator being dropped on my back. Someone was gripping tightly around my neck, forcing me underwater and making me inhale lungfuls of water. Without panic or hesitation, I pulled three hard strokes, bringing us to the bottom of the pool. I felt a gag reflex coming from my throat as a result of the water I'd breathed in, but I forced myself to remain focused on my task.

I could feel the survivor struggling to get to the surface, so I bent forward, loosening his hold, and grabbed his arm, which was wrapped around my neck. I pulled straight down to break his hold. Meanwhile, I gripped his wrist with my right hand and slid my left hand to his elbow. My fingers landed on the pressure point, and I heard a painful exhalation of bubbles escape from the survivor's mouth. I rotated his arm over my head, released his elbow, and locked him in a cross-chest carry with his wrist still pinned behind his back. I kicked my fins hard to propel both of us to the surface, where we took in some much-needed air. I kept a strong grip as I forced the water from my lungs in exchange for oxygen. Looking left to right to ensure my path was clear, I saw the instructor slowly nodding his head and giving a thumbs-up. I'd passed lifesaving.

And without realizing it, I'd gotten some invaluable preparation for being on a mountain one day, where focus is a life-or-death issue. Gratefully, I made it down the mountain safely and without incident. I planned to rest at base camp for a few days before heading back up to Camp I.

On Easter, I called JoAnna. I knew that she and the kids would be having dinner with friends back home.

"Hi, honey!" JoAnna said. "Let me put you on speaker so you can talk to everyone."

I was met with a chorus of greetings from the kids and from our friends. "How are you doing?" they asked.

"Great!" I said. "I'm about to head up to Camp I through the Khumbu Icefall. How's everybody back home?"

Just as they started to respond, I saw that Pasang was gathering our supplies. "I'm so sorry," I said. "I have to hurry up and get moving. Happy Easter!"

Then I talked directly to JoAnna. "I love you, sweetie. Tell the kids I love them too."

"Be careful," she said, as she always does. "We love you!"

•

Before we began our trip, Bill and I had agreed to climb on our own schedules. We would stay together when possible, but neither of us wanted to feel like he was impeding the other person's success. Since Bill had been sick, he was now one day behind me in the acclimatization process. Pasang was pulling double duty, heading back to Camp I with me and then returning to base camp to help Bill. That meant I'd be spending the night alone at Camp I. I planned to continue up to Camp II with Lakpa the next day, and then we'd descend all the way back to base camp. This would push my body to adapt to higher elevations and then force it to produce more red blood cells when I rested back at base camp.

That morning's climb through the Khumbu Icefall was uneventful, and I could tell I was stronger than I'd been my first time through. I didn't get winded throughout the entire trek to Camp I, even though my pack was heavier this time. I was now transporting my high-altitude gear, which consisted of my –40-degree sleeping bag and my down suit. Although the down suit was awkward to carry with me, I knew I'd be grateful to have it once we got nearer to Camp II. The suit covered my entire body and was made of 850-fill down feathers, which made it essentially like walking around in a sleeping bag.

As we walked, Pasang monitored my progress. "You are very strong," he told me. "You should only need to go to Camp II once to sleep. Then you can climb to Camp III."

My mind was racing: *After that, I'll sleep on supplemental oxygen at Camp III . . . and then I'll be ready for the summit!*

Halfway through the icefall, we crossed paths with Dave Hahn, who was leading a group for a Seattle-based guiding company.

"Hey, Dave, how's it going?" I shook his hand, both of us still in our climbing gloves. "I'm your Everest base camp neighbor."

"Hey, man! We're just coming down from our first rotation at Camp II."

"That's great," I said. "Have a safe trip." I made my way to the next ladder and clipped into the fixed line.

"See you at camp," he said as he headed back to check on his clients.

I didn't mind the quietness of the climb with just Pasang and me, but it was nice to see another friendly face along the way.

With the recent avalanches and the seracs that had collapsed from Lola Peak, the icefall had already changed since I was there just a few days earlier. When I arrived at one of the crevasses, I saw that it had widened, requiring four ladders instead of three. That may not seem like much, but with each additional ladder, the platform becomes increasingly unstable. I started across one of the newly expanded crevasses, and with each step I took, I could feel the ladders dipping down with the weight of my body. I felt the entire temporary bridge swaying slightly, first to the left and then to the right. I was relieved to step off the ladders and onto the slightly more stable ground.

It wasn't long before we came to a couple of sections where we'd need to do some ice climbing. These spots would have been easier with ladders, but we'd have to make do without. We squeezed through tight ice walls and front pointed our crampons to climb over the looming seracs. I was grateful I had the right gear for this. My crampons had come equipped with steel spikes on the front (front points), which I forced into the ice for stability. Essentially I was relying on my foot protection to hold me as I used anchored ropes to haul myself up a 15-foot wall of ice. I could only imagine the horrific damage that could occur if I was in the wrong place at the wrong time under one of those massive ice blocks.

At one point, when I was crossing a two-section ladder and standing on the third rung, a Sherpa accidentally let go of my fixed rope handle. I lost my balance and stepped backward off the ladder. As I stepped back, my crampons struck the shin of one of the Sherpas who was standing behind me. I felt awful and bent down to look at his leg and make sure he was okay. Thankfully, his skin had barely been punctured.

"I'm fine," he assured me with a smile. "It wasn't your fault."

When we got to Camp I, Pasang boiled water for hot tea, and we ate a boxed lunch of meat, cheese, fruit, and bread. As I was setting up my tent, he dropped off a few propane stoves, fuel, and food for future meals since I'd be cooking on my own after he headed back down the mountain. I was glad to have a handheld radio in case something went wrong, but I wasn't really concerned about my solo camping adventure.

Before Pasang descended, I had an important question to ask him. "Is there a safe place to use the restroom?"

Everything was pretty exposed at the top of the icefall, with nothing but seracs and open crevasses surrounding the tent.

"Yes." He pointed toward the icefall. "Be careful!" Then he disappeared into the river of falling ice.

I set up my tripod and filmed myself doing some interior decorating in my tent—blowing up my inflatable mattress and setting out my sleeping bag. I wanted to document my journey for my family so they would have at least some idea of what this experience was like. I managed to inflate the mattress without passing out or getting light headed, so that seemed like a good sign. However, it did take considerable effort just to set up my tent and get my sleeping area ready— something I wouldn't have even noticed at lower altitudes. That's high altitude for you—simple tasks take triple the effort.

After I drank a few liters of water, it was time to break the seal and depart from my cozy tent so I could explore the area Pasang had pointed out. Just three steps away from my tent vestibule was a step-over crevasse that was so deep I couldn't even see the bottom. I could see how someone who fell into that crack in the middle of the night would never be heard from again. To prevent injury, I grabbed a bamboo wand with a piece of red tape on the end—a makeshift flag—to mark the danger. I also dropped off an empty Gatorade bottle at my tent so I wouldn't have to venture out in the darkness if I needed to relieve myself. I walked toward the other tents to find a narrow area to cross and eventually found a spot that functioned as a primitive outhouse.

After returning to my tent, I realized I was ravenous, so I ate some trail mix and a candy bar. I ticked off the most common symptoms of acute mountain sickness in my head: headache, nausea, lack of appetite. I was eating enough food for three people, which I took to be a good sign. My metabolism was burning through food almost as quickly as I could chew it, so I continued indulging in carbs and fats.

Since I had some downtime in the afternoon, I decided to get some film footage for my sponsors. I brought my tripod, camera, and mini-high-definition video recorder and tried to get video with Everest in the background. After I started filming, I noticed that some of the climbers who were camping 30 yards below me had come out of their tents to watch me record myself. I wasn't expecting an audience, so the attention made me a little nervous. I did a few takes and figured I could edit them later. The wind was picking up, and the temperature was dropping, so I wrapped up and returned to my tent.

I'd brought along a sealed card from JoAnna and the kids to open on Easter. It seemed like so long ago that I'd talked to them, even though it had been earlier that morning. There was something about knowing it was a holiday that made me miss my family even more than usual. I opened the card in the solitude of my tent.

Happy Easter! We are so proud of you. We miss you, and we can't wait for you to come home. We love you so much!

Love,
JoAnna, Emily, and Jordan

Tears streamed down my face as I sat there alone, wishing with almost every part of my being that I could be home to celebrate with them. But I quickly realized that crying in the high altitude created intense pressure on my head, so I willed my tears to stop.

The wind outside picked up, and I could feel the wind thrashing my tent, so I decided to stay inside and watch *The Empire Strikes Back* on my mini-laptop. It was a much-needed distraction to lose myself in a story other than my own for a few hours. I bundled up in several warm layers, snuggled into my —40-degree sleeping bag, and finally drifted off to sleep.

•

The higher elevation dramatically affected my body's chemistry and fluid balance—a condition called altitude diuresis—which meant I had to get up four times that night to empty my bladder. The urine in the bottle froze almost immediately, which made for an interesting night. After each use, I had to melt and pour out the contents a few feet from the tent so the bottle would be ready for the next time I woke up.

When I awoke at 5 a.m., it took me a moment to remember where I was. Then reality came charging into my consciousness: I was at Camp I on Mount Everest!

I packed my gear, lit the stove, and boiled some melted

snow for coffee (I was careful to make sure it was the non-yellow variety). Then it was time to prepare my freeze-dried breakfast: two bags of seafood noodles and one kimchi noodle package. As I forced down the last few bites, Lakpa showed up with supplies for Camp II. He had a cast-iron cooking stove and a couple of oxygen bottles strapped to his back, which likely totaled more than 100 pounds. I had been expecting him to arrive at eight o'clock, and it was only seven. *How does he do it?* I marveled. I quickly got my things together, and five minutes later we were on the trail.

The route to Camp II wasn't too difficult, as it followed the Western Cwm for a couple of miles, up to 21,300 feet. We negotiated across a handful of ladders, most of which we crossed uneventfully. We did encounter one crevasse that was so wide it required five ladders tied together, end to end. There was, however, an optional 15-minute walk-around, and I usually took that route. I crossed the five-ladder crevasse only once to get a picture. The moment I stepped on the first ladder, it dropped about a foot and started swinging from side to side. With each shaky step, I had to balance by gripping the safety lines and taking slow, deliberate steps while keeping my eyes fixed on each rung. Beneath me I saw hundreds of feet of glacial blue ice that disappeared into a deep, black abyss.

Through the rest of the Western Cwm, Lakpa and I moved efficiently, which is the term for "fast" in mountaineering, but for the last half hour of our journey to Camp II, it felt like we were in slow motion. I felt fine physically and wasn't having trouble breathing, but even so, at that altitude, your pack feels heavier and your body moves more slowly.

For the first time the whole trip, I saw Sherpas stopping

to catch their breath. *They're human after all*, I thought. It felt frustrating not to keep up a fast, long stride and a steady pace, but it was a good opportunity to practice my rest step—not to mention patience.

The rest step feels unnatural, and it requires a conscious effort to take a step, shift your weight, and pause for three seconds before taking another step. But I knew it was the wise thing to do if I was going to reach my destination. Instead of counting to three during the pause, I silently recited the names of my family: *Emily, Jordan, JoAnna*. Step. *Emily, Jordan, JoAnna*. This mantra gave me a constant reminder of my priorities, and in some small way, it felt like they were there with me, cheering me on.

One of the things that often surprises people about climbing is how intense the solitude can be. That's one of the draws for me, because in the mountains, the constant chaos and distractions of life are stripped away. The silence at high altitudes is so profound it can seem almost deafening at times. The quiet is broken only by the occasional gust of wind or the sound of distant avalanches and falling ice. It's a powerful way to reset the mind, but it can also push climbers to the tipping point between sanity and insanity.

The positive side of being away from family is that it helps you appreciate them more—but that can also be the negative side. Some climbers abandon their goal partway through out of intense homesickness, and then after returning home, they wish they'd stuck it out and taken the opportunity they'd been saving for and training for.

I could feel myself teetering on that brink as I climbed, torn between missing my family and wanting to accomplish this goal I'd been striving toward. I thought about the

six-month deployments I'd endured in the Navy. I'd done
two stints in the Persian Gulf—one in 1995 and the second
in 1997. Those six-month deployments felt long, crammed
onto a carrier with 5,000 other people. The only things that
got me through were faith and focus. Each day was different based on the missions we were assigned, but I tried
to stick to a routine as much as I could: workouts, meals,
training, college courses (which I took on the ship), and
prayer. It also helped to dream about the future and plan
things JoAnna and I would do together once I returned to
the States. I tried to use those same strategies now—keeping
a consistent routine and remembering who was waiting for
me back home.

Camp II is located at the base of Lhotse Face. From camp
you can look straight up and see Camp III, the Yellow Band,
the South Col, the South Summit, and the true summit. It
didn't look like any of the pictures I'd seen because I was at
such close range. From this vantage point, the peak looked
deceptively attainable. But then I took a slow walk across
camp, and I was brought back to reality. I realized that I still
had about two miles of vertical feet to go, and at this slow-
motion rate, that sounded like a long distance.

As I made my way into our cooking tent, Lakpa smiled
and said, "Brian, you are strong. Like a Sherpa without a
client!" I was flattered—not just because of his words but
because of the source. This was coming from someone whose
people were the strongest climbers in the world.

After tea, spicy noodles, and a short rest, we packed up
to head down again. The descent through the Western Cwm
was similar to the Muir snowfield on Mount Rainier, which
I'd climbed countless times back home. The terrain was flat

and descended gradually, so I was able to step up my pace. I almost wished I'd brought my snowboard along so I could bomb my way down in a few minutes flat!

Back at Camp I, I stuffed my remaining gear into my backpack and rehydrated. I chatted with Bill and Pasang for a few minutes while Lakpa and another Sherpa continued ahead of me. Then I carefully moved out of Camp I across the multiple crevasses. I caught up with both Sherpas and started walking with them. They picked up the pace, and I did my best to keep up. We ended up making record time through the icefall, returning to base camp in just two hours.

I had to stay at Everest base camp for the next four days to acclimatize, and I knew that being inactive for so long could be one of the most maddening parts of the trip for me. After so many days of intense physical activity, my efforts came screeching to a halt.

I thought back to my days of SERE training. As challenging as the physical tests were, the mental drills were even more intense. One of the segments of our training was sustaining enemy torture. We spent two days in a mock POW camp, where physical and mental interrogation tactics were used on us, including waterboarding. We were marched for more than a mile to the "prisoner camp" and placed in individual boxes with dank-smelling canvas sacks over our heads. We had to sit in a specific upright position—with our legs crossed and our arms extended, and with our elbows resting on our knees. It was an incredibly uncomfortable position that caused almost immediate cramping. All through the day and night, we were accosted by the blaring sounds of repetitive music, dripping water, and the crying of babies. The intention was to break us down mentally.

We were brought into interrogation rooms and tortured to find out how far we would go before we broke and gave up classified information. Then we were tempted with a softer approach—in a comfortable room with attractive female interrogators. Our mission was to resist and stick to the code of conduct, no matter the approach—even and especially when the enemy wasn't adhering to the rules.

At one point I was pulled into a room, slapped, and slammed against the wall. Then I was locked in a small box, which was barely large enough for me to fit in. Later, when the door was opened, they found me fast asleep—utterly unfazed. I was yanked out and given another round of beatings and then brought back to my main box with the others.

After a week of misery, an American flag was raised and the national anthem was played, indicating that we had been rescued and were heading home. We stood at attention, many of us with tears streaming down our cheeks. I'd lost about 15 pounds in a matter of days due to lack of food and the stress of the interrogations.

If I could survive a week of hearing the constant sound of dripping water in my cell, I told myself, *I can handle a few days of rest at base camp.*

On the first rest day, I decided to do some much-needed laundry. A base camp Sherpa brought out two bowls of hot water—one large and one small. As soon as I doused my soiled clothing, it began to snow. I quickly washed, rinsed, and repeated until the water was a disgusting shade of brown. I rigged a line between the tents with some climbing cord so I could hang my clothes.

After eating lunch in our dining tent, I returned to find my clothes frozen solid, with 6- to 10-inch icicles hanging from them. I had to be careful since the clothes would easily snap if I mishandled them—I didn't have much in the way of wardrobe options. I brought my clothes inside the tent and allowed them to slowly thaw out for the next two days. Even after my clothes were washed and dried, they didn't feel clean or comfortable like they would back home after cycling through my indoor front-load washer and dryer.

The next day the weather turned relatively warm, so after two weeks of not showering, I decided to use the opportunity to get clean (or at least cleaner). It took four Sherpas to haul barrels of water and pound on the electrical heating device, but they finally got it working. It felt like heaven! After so many days of baby-wipe baths, my greasy hair had reached a point where it could stand up in any direction with a gentle comb of my hand. After a couple of shampoo treatments and a good rinse, I might as well have been Fabio, whipping my tender, brown locks in slow motion from side to side in the shower tent. Who would have ever guessed that being clean would be such a major morale boost?

•

I used the rest days to catch up my blog entries. I wrote them in the warmth of my tent and then hiked 30 minutes outside of camp to my "Internet cafe" to post them. There was a lot of press that year about how there would be 3G Internet coverage at Everest base camp for the first time, but when I arrived, I found that that assessment wasn't entirely accurate. It was true that Nepal's 3G service provided coverage from Gorak Shep, a village a few miles down the Khumbu Valley. The 3G towers were powered by walls of solar panels, but they were spotty in bad weather, and at night they were shut down to conserve power. We could have worked around those limitations, but the worst part was that the towers weren't strong enough to send a 3G signal into base camp. We received EDGE coverage, which was sufficient for cell phone calls, but it was unreliable for Internet access.

To upload blog entries, send e-mails, add pictures to social media sites, or make video calls, I had to hike 30 minutes out of base camp and climb out onto a ridge. I would sit on a large, flat boulder, which was the only place I'd found where I could get fairly consistent coverage. The view from the rock was breathtaking. From that vantage point, I could see the icefall crawling down the mountain, the summit of Mount Everest, and the surrounding Himalayan peaks.

I tried to schedule my calls for times when JoAnna and the kids were awake, which ended up being the start of my day and the end of theirs. I was 12 hours and 45 minutes ahead of the time zone back home in Washington, and I was glad to have my time conversion spreadsheet. Prior to my trip, I'd mapped out the time differences between home and Everest, and it was handy not to have to recalculate each time I called.

One morning as I sat on the rock trying to get the Internet to load up, I thought, *I've been away from my family for a whole month now.* That caused a lump to form in my throat, but it was motivating to think about how close I was to reaching my goal. *It won't be long before I'm home again,* I coached myself.

Not only was I eager to see my family, but I was also ready to eat some real food again. At first the food had been interesting and part of the adventure, and I'd tried to make the most of it. But by now, I dreaded each mealtime. It wasn't

April 1, 1997, San Diego, California. Saying good-bye to JoAnna before flying out to the USS Constellation aircraft carrier for a six-month deployment.

The Persian Gulf doing some aerial gunner training during Operation Southern Watch (1997).

Being lowered into the Pacific Ocean from the SH-60F Seahawk (1997).

April 1, 2011, Bangkok, Thailand. Rolling 200 pounds of expedition gear (mine and my climbing partner's) to the check-in counter to get our tickets to Kathmandu, Nepal.

Flying from Kathmandu to Lukla in the Khumbu Valley. I was surprised to see the main pilot reading the newspaper instead of watching the 20,000-foot peak surrounding the plane.

In Lukla, Nepal, trekking toward Phakding, the first village we stayed in during our trek to Everest base camp. Notice the animal photobombing in the back with its tongue out. It's called a dzo—a cross between a yak and a cow.

Kathmandu, Nepal, handing out toys to the children of the Early Childhood Development Center.

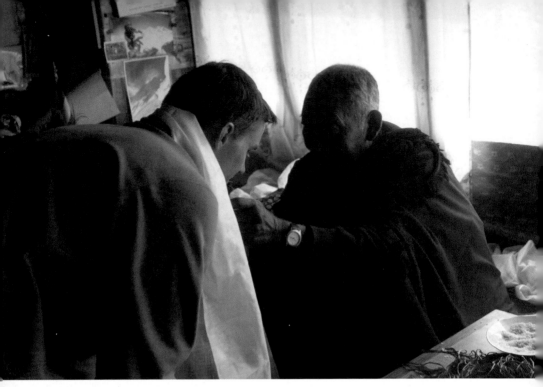

Lama Geshi placing a white silk scarf around my neck for good luck at the end of a puja ceremony.

Taking an acclimatization hike during a rest day in Namche Bazaar (the village is below me).

On April 11, nearly two weeks after leaving home, we finally arrived at Everest base camp (17,500 feet), our home away from home for the next couple of months.

On April 21, Pasang (pictured) and I climbed through the Khumbu Icefall to reach Camp I (19,700 feet) before descending back to base camp as part of our acclimatization process.

Crossing five ladders over a crevasse in the Western Cwm.

On April 25, Lakpa and I climbed up to Camp II (21,300 feet), where we had lunch and then descended to base camp to rest for a few days before heading up to Camp III.

I took this shot on May 14 while ascending the Geneva Spur toward the South Col. The arrow indicates climbers who were descending from a summit attempt. Most climbers turned back near the South Summit that day due to high winds.

Relaxing at Camp III (23,700 feet) the day before my summit attempt. Small shelves are cut into the side of the steep Lhotse Face to anchor tents to the mountain.

May 14, halfway between Camp III (23,700 feet) and the South Col (26,000 feet). I took this selfie after retrieving my dropped goggles. Notice the crack down the center of the internal lens and the condensation and ice that started to form between the layers.

This panoramic shot was taken from the summit of Mount Everest (29,035 feet) with a view of Lhotse (the fourth-tallest mountain in the world).

I took this selfie on the summit of Mount Everest moments before going snow blind. Below is another picture I took more than seven hours later, after reaching the South Col. My eyes were pretty much swollen shut and completely useless throughout the descent. They wouldn't return to normal for another month and a half.

Summit (29,035 feet)

South Summit (28,700 feet)

South Rock Step

Pasang turned back

Balcony (27,500 feet)

Ran out of oxygen

South Col (26,000 feet)

Pasang met me on my
way into the South Col

This map shows my final summit push and descent routes.

JoAnna, Emily, Jordan, and me in the Canadian Rockies in June 2013.

our cook's fault—I was eating plenty, and he was doing a good job considering the limited access he had to fresh food, refrigeration, and cooking appliances. But after so many consecutive days of eating Spam and dal bhat (a Nepalese curry dish consisting of rice and lentils), I was ready for a nice big cheeseburger, a steak, a Starbucks Caramel Macchiato—anything, really. I was even looking forward to the flight food we'd get from Thai Airways on the way home. It wasn't even the food itself that I craved; it was the freedom to be able to get whatever I wanted, whenever I wanted it. I had to force myself not to lie in my tent and dream of food back home, since I knew that would only depress me more.

While I didn't want to dwell on food, I couldn't resist posting this entry on *Climbing* magazine's blog.

April 28, 2011

If someone could please drop ship a carne asada burrito from Roberto's in San Diego or a Double-Double Animal Style from In-n-Out Burger, I sure would appreciate it![1]

Almost daily I heard the *thump* of helicopter blades as another person was evacuated from base camp. Some climbers were facing life-threatening high-altitude problems, such as excess fluids in the lungs or cerebral edema. In other cases, clients paid a cool $5,000 to get a quick ride out of a dream that had turned into a nightmare.

Finally, after four days at base camp, it was time to head up to Camp III to finalize our acclimatization process. On April 30, Bill, Veronique, her two Sherpas, Pasang, and I climbed up the Khumbu Icefall to Camp I, where we would spend the night. Our little group spread out as we climbed at our own pace. My pace was getting faster, since the terrain was now a lot more familiar to me. Although the mountain was constantly changing, I knew where certain hazards were and recognized various crevasses. One area had been wiped out by a falling serac, and now instead of having horizontal ladder crossings, there were vertical ladders we used to climb down into the crevasse, hike across the bottom, and then go back up the ladders to get out.

I made my way up through the icefall and turned the corner above the mass of ice sculptures to see a cluster of yellow and orange tents. I'd made it to Camp I. While I waited for the others, I fired up the stoves to melt snow, which we'd use to replenish our water bottles. Then I set up the tent Bill and I would share at the top of Camp I and got to work stowing all my sharp items (crampons, ice axe, poles, and pickets) outside the tent. Once everyone else added their gear to the cache with mine, we'd mark it with a bamboo wand and a flag. That way if a snowfall came overnight and our gear got buried, we'd be able to find it quickly.

I woke up early the next morning, eager to get moving. The rest of the group wasn't ready yet, and my toes were getting cold, so I set out for Camp II a little earlier than the others. I listened to my headphones and kept my head up, taking in the beautiful 360-degree views. The climb felt smooth, and before I knew it I was at Camp II.

We spent two nights at Camp II, also known as advance base camp (ABC). The setup at Camp II was similar to Everest base camp, with individual tents, a bathroom tent, and a dining tent staffed by our amazing cook, Dawa, who always served us with a smile. He made great fried potatoes and pancakes; plus, he usually had a can of Pringles, which always hit the spot! Like most of the other Sherpas, he had a family back home that worried about his high-altitude job.

"Dawa, you are a very good cook," I told him. "But does your wife wish you'd do something else that's less dangerous?" I asked.

Dawa's face broke into a contagious smile. "I want to climb Mount Everest someday."

•

Later that evening, Mount Everest claimed its first victim of the year on the south side. One of the climbers had experienced a severe case of edema a few days prior, shortly after his summit attempt. He had collapsed when he was nearing Camp III and died almost instantly. News travels quickly through the Sherpa community, but at this point we didn't have any way to verify what we'd heard. I later learned that this climber's name was Rick Hitch, and he was from California. It was strange to be cut off from media access, knowing that people back home likely had more information than we did about something that had happened just a few hundred yards away from us.

We were taking the south route up Everest, through Nepal—the same route Rick had taken. It's probably a pretty even split between climbers who take the south route and those who take the north route. More deaths have occurred on the north side, but there are many different variables that have contributed to those fatalities, and the risks run about equal on both sides. The north route is easier at the lower sections but slightly more dangerous higher up due to the extreme winds and colder temperatures, plus the technically difficult Second Step, which is a straight-up ladder climb at 28,000 feet. There's also no chance of helicopter rescue on the north route. The south route is difficult since you have to traverse the Khumbu Icefall, which is arguably the most dangerous area on either side due to the constant falling hazards. Plus, there's the long summit night and the Cornice Traverse, with its nearly two-mile drop on each side.

The next day we walked by a tent just 200 yards from our camp. The tent was windblown and eerily lifeless, and it took a moment for it to dawn on me that it had belonged to Rick. They had temporarily stashed his body there until the rest of the group descended. I couldn't help but wonder if I'd have been able to help him survive if I'd been closer, but I suppose that was all the search-and-rescue training in me.

Training to become an air rescue swimmer is intense—approximately 60 percent of candidates drop out or are asked to leave. But for me the challenges were worth it. There's something compelling about the duty of risking your own life to save someone else. The AIRR motto is simply, "So others may live." As rescuers, we didn't really think about the sacrifice involved—we just took off in search of people in need. Now we were in the mountains, not over the ocean, but the same sobering truth remained: life is fragile.

The following day we watched a couple of climbers being taken on a helicopter recovery mission from the base of Lhotse Face. We heard that several other climbers were evacuated down the mountain with oxygen, while another client fell on the bergschrund—a massive ice formation that separates from the mountain—and reportedly broke his wrists.

That's not the kind of news you like to hear at 21,000 feet above the ground.

"Lord, please bring healing and peace to those who are leaving today," I prayed. "And please comfort Rick's family, wherever they are."

I knew JoAnna would worry if she heard the news about the fatality and wonder if I'd been hurt. I didn't have cell coverage at higher elevations, so I borrowed Veronique's satellite phone.

"Hi, honey!" JoAnna said when she heard my voice. Her voice echoed with the time delay.

"Hey, sweetie. I'm borrowing a satellite phone, so I need to be quick. There was a reported death, but I wanted to let you know that my whole team is fine. I didn't want you to worry."

"Thanks for letting me know," she said. "I miss you. The kids miss you. But we're staying busy. Yesterday—"

"Honey, I'm sorry, but it's not my phone. I have to go, but I'll call you in a few days. I'm heading up to Camp III and then I'll be back at base camp. Don't worry—I'll be safe."

I hated to cut her off and not hear about what she and the kids were doing, but I knew how expensive satellite minutes were, and I didn't want to abuse the favor. After all, I might need to ask again.

"I love you," JoAnna said. "Please be safe."

As I hung up, I thought about the anxiety JoAnna had experienced when I was preparing to climb Denali. Our church was doing the Soul Revolution challenge at the time—a 60-day challenge to help us align our thinking with Christ. We both had little timers that went off each hour throughout the day as a simple reminder to pause and connect with Christ.

The challenge just happened to fall during my two-and-a-half-week expedition on Denali, and it helped to know we were both going through the same thing even though we were so far apart physically. We felt connected to one another through Christ, and it helped JoAnna get over her anxiety to remember that God was watching over both of us. It helped me, too, reminding me that no matter how many miles away I was, God was protecting my family. I hoped that same sense of closeness with Christ was sustaining her now.

•

The following day we packed up and began our climb to Camp III. The weather fluctuated from cold to colder, and then, out of nowhere, we'd hit pockets of air that were insanely hot. But by the time I'd strip down a layer, it was freezing again. I had my full down suit on at Camp II, and then when the sun hit the ice, I started overheating, so I dropped the suit down halfway, tying the arms around my waist. I wanted to be careful not to overheat, as I knew that would drain my energy quickly. And if I was sweating and it suddenly got cold, I could put myself at risk for hypothermia. I was glad to have layers and clothing with side zippers for ventilation.

Bill and I made it from Camp II to the base of Lhotse Face within an hour. At 27,940 feet, Lhotse is the fourth-highest mountain in the world. To climb Mount Everest's south side, you have to climb halfway up Lhotse before cutting over to the South Col. The entire climb up Lhotse is intense, as it's essentially a vertical sheet of ice and snow.

After taking a couple of minutes to rest, I connected myself to the fixed lines and headed up the ice wall. I was surprised to see that some of the climbers weren't connected to the fixed lines, but I didn't want to take unnecessary chances. The only time I disconnected was when I transitioned between pickets or ice screws, and even then I only disconnected one device at a time so that if I slipped, I wouldn't fall farther than my other device. If you slip on Lhotse Face, you won't stop for thousands of feet, which translates into certain death. This is no place for climber's ego—after all, there's no shame in surviving!

There were two side-by-side options for fixed lines, and climbers were heading up and down both of them. This created challenges when climbers tried to maneuver around each other on the icy surface. There was also the danger of falling ice or rocks that could descend from above, so we had to be alert at all times.

We were all heading up at our own pace, and at one point I looked around to see where the other climbers in the group were. Bill was a few hundred yards below me, but I had no idea where Veronique and her two Sherpas were. They'd gotten a later start from Camp II and planned to meet us on the ice ledge for a night's rest. Although Bill had experienced some nausea down below, he was moving strong up the fixed lines. His method of interval bursts was working well for him. Meanwhile, I was continuing my steady three-second cadence: *Emily, Jordan, JoAnna.* Step. *Emily, Jordan, JoAnna.* Step.

This was one of the hardest climbing days I'd had so far. As I made my way up the vertical sheet of ice, I thought about my move to high camp on Mount McKinley several years before. I'd been carrying 70 pounds with me, and I was fighting 60-mile-per-hour winds. Severe wind is one of the biggest mental challenges you can face on a climb. Not only does it cut through your clothes, freezing you to the core, but it also is so loud it can prevent you from communicating with others on your team. Fierce winds tend to kick up violent drifts of snow and ice, making it difficult to see and filling your clothing with ice. And perhaps most of all, windy conditions require you to stay mentally sharp as you strain to keep your balance against the forceful gusts. In those situations, the only thing to do is stay calm and press on, one foot in front of the other, until you reach your destination.

The final hundred yards up to Camp III were slow and painful. By this time I was taking five-second pauses between steps and using more of my upper body to jumar up the line. Each muscle in my body felt like it was being crushed by 100-pound weights. I felt paralyzed as I forced my feet to take each step. And it wasn't just my muscles that were spent; I was mentally exhausted as well. Everything felt like it was in slow motion—my movements, my thoughts, and my reactions. I had also fueled out and was in desperate need of food, but it was too dangerous to anchor off to find a place to eat, so I had to power through.

Finally, about a mile up Lhotse Face, I got a glimpse of tents anchored to the side of the ice wall. Camp III wasn't much to speak of—it was basically just a peppering of about 20 tents—but at that moment it was one of the happiest sights I'd ever seen. I was about 30 yards away, which would take about half an hour at this rate, but I knew I was going to make it.

After three hours of climbing, Bill and I finally made it to the tents, where we fell onto our sleeping bags. Eventually I forced myself to do the work—and it was work—of removing my boots and harness. I lay there basking in the satisfaction of another mission accomplished.

That feeling of exhaustion mixed with satisfaction was a little like what I'd felt when I passed the basic requirements of Naval training after an agonizing six months. One of my classmates and I earned our Aircrew wings on the same day— the gold wings we'd wear on our uniforms above the medals and ribbons. But before we were able to get our wings, the other Aircrew members conducted a time-tested hazing ritual. After forcing us to drink a pitcher of beer each, they took off the backings of the pins and pierced the two points straight into our chests. Then each Aircrew member stood in a line and, with all their strength, punched them deeper into our skin until the posts were bent. I still have the scars. As I stood there with my fellow Aircrew men, I was bloody and sore, but also proud. I had earned my "blood wings" and more important, I had accomplished the goal I'd set out to achieve.

I sank into my sleeping bag and relaxed, not thinking about anything. At that altitude, every minor task—even thinking—takes a tremendous amount of energy. My plan for the evening was to eat dinner and then sleep using supplemental oxygen.

Veronique and her climbing Sherpa made it to Camp III an hour after we arrived, and they settled into the tent next to us. I congratulated her through the tent wall but didn't hear a response. I imagined she was as exhausted as Bill and I were.

As I prepared a dinner (chicken soup and spicy noodle soup, plus a BOUNTY bar for dessert), I looked out of our tent at the view from our little platform. We were on a small ice shelf just large enough for the two-man tents. The shelf was cold and windy, not to mention impossibly steep. It had been cut out of a 55-degree slope that fell straight down for a mile to the Western Cwm. The Sherpas had chosen our tent location carefully and made sure the safety lines were tight to ensure that no mishaps would occur. I was glad we were anchored in, as a fall would mean certain death.

Camp III is a notoriously dangerous area to camp. Many climbers have been lost after going outside their tents to use the bathroom without crampons or some form of safety rope to catch their fall. I looked down from my tent and shook my head. If you slipped, you'd go for a ride for thousands of feet down—no chance of survival.

In the distance I could see Cho Oyu, the sixth-highest mountain in the world. Camp II was straight below, with Camp I so far in the distance that it was hard to see. Behind us was Lhotse Face, and off to the left was the South Summit of Everest.

Just before dinner, Pasang came in to inform us that one of the oxygen regulators was broken. Since I felt the best altitude-wise, I volunteered to go without oxygen for the night, but Bill wouldn't hear of it. Pasang suggested we open a bottle of oxygen in the tent without a regulator or mask. That didn't seem like the best solution, though, since the tent walls were thin and anything we pumped in would easily escape. I insisted that I was fine and told Pasang to get some food for himself. After about an hour Pasang returned to our tent with a borrowed regulator from another climbing team's staged gear, which he would replace at Camp II. He configured my mask for a one-liter-per-minute flow. Although I felt confident I would have been fine without oxygen, I was relieved to have it just in case. I wore my mask at a low-flow rate all through the night.

I felt the effects of supplemental oxygen almost immediately. It filled my body with warmth and gave me energy and life. It was almost like going down in elevation for the night. But as good as the oxygen felt, it was awkward to sleep with something attached to my face. While I slept, everything around me became frozen and frost covered except me. Inside my face mask, condensation formed, meaning that water dripped on my face every few seconds during the night. Even so, it was worth the price to be able to breathe easily.

Bill and I woke at 5 a.m. and started preparing for our descent back to Everest base camp. I had a high-definition video camera mounted to my helmet to try to get some descent footage, but it froze immediately due to the cold temperatures and wind. It didn't thaw out until the next day when we reached a lower elevation.

I alternated rappelling Australian style (head first) and backward down Lhotse Face, and I reached Camp II in about 45 minutes. We had a breakfast of potatoes and pancakes prepared by Dawa, and I then set out on my own all the way to base camp. I was eager to breathe in the thick air again and complete my acclimatization process.

We were almost there. It was hard to wrap my mind around how much our bodies had adjusted to the elevation, but it put things in perspective when I realized that if our plane lost cabin pressure on the way home and the oxygen masks fell from the ceiling, we wouldn't need to put them on.

The next stop was the death zone, where the body can't acclimate and starts to wither away and die, even with supplemental oxygen. But I was ready. The next move up the mountain would be for the summit attempt!

CHAPTER 6

EYEING THE MOUNTAIN

I lift up my eyes to the mountains—where does my help come from?
My help comes from the LORD, the Maker of heaven and earth.

PSALM 121:1-2

MAY 5, 2011

Since our acclimatization process is complete, we will
rest at base camp and wait for a weather window for
a summit attempt. Some groups are trying to summit
on the seventh, but we've had so much snow lately
that the fixed lines above the South Col aren't in
place. We don't want to risk having the Sherpas hurry
to set the lines and then have to change them later.
On this mountain, patience is necessary for a safe
and successful climb.

We were right on schedule to be one of the earlier groups
to make an attempt on the summit. But I didn't want to rush

anything, especially with the recent snowfall. As much as I wanted to summit, I was committed to being safe and making wise choices. Climbing Mount Everest isn't just about skill and strategic planning—there's also patience and some luck involved. No amount of preparation can help you if the weather doesn't cooperate once you've acclimatized and are ready to make your final ascent. I was glad that part of my mental preparation for the trip had been focusing on returning home safely, no matter the outcome of the climb.

Pasang, Bill, and I talked through our plan for the final summit push. It would take five days to get into position at high camp from Everest base camp, and we'd have to hope for a weather window shortly after we arrived. We planned out our route, which looked pretty straightforward on paper, but we knew it was possible to run into any number of variables, such as inclement weather, injury, and other unknowns.

I wonder how my body will perform as we head to the top, I thought as I sat at base camp, waiting to head to high camp. Granted, there was something to be said for familiarity. It gave me confidence to know I'd done part of this journey before so I had some idea of what to expect along the way. But there was one key piece I'd never experienced before: the death zone. *How will I do in that fierce unknown?*

There was only one way to find out.

I called JoAnna every day while we waited to set out for high camp, getting caught up on what she and the kids were doing. When I was back in my tent, I rehearsed every detail of the plan until it felt as familiar as reciting my home address. It wasn't long before I was tired of thinking about the plan and just wanted to execute it—ready or not. If

I was capable of handling the challenge, I would feel the thrill of success. If not, I would come back and live to climb another day.

During my six years in the military, I learned that it's up to you to do everything you can do to be prepared, and then at some point you just have to do your best and trust God to handle everything else. This was especially true when our crew did tours in the Persian Gulf, where we flew daily missions. During our six-month tours, I lost an average of two Aircrew buddies a year due to training mishaps.

During one night flight in the middle of the Pacific, while the crew was wearing night-vision goggles, the pilots became disoriented and flew into the ocean during their approach to the carrier. The forward g-force of the impact killed everyone on board instantly, and the helicopter sank to the bottom of the ocean. Another time, during a combat search-and-rescue training flight, the helo crashed into the side of a steep cliff, killing the crew as they rolled into a ravine. Their bodies were burned and charred to the seats, which had to be cut out by fellow Aircrewmen.

I experienced some close calls myself. We were flying a VERTREP (vertical replenishment) mission just outside Japan, with the assignment of off-loading tons of weapons onto a carrier. We had 5,000 pounds hanging from a hook 20 feet below the helicopter when the carrier disappeared into a whiteout fog. We couldn't see our hands in front of our faces, and we quickly lost sight of the carrier. Vertigo set in, but the pilots fell back on their training and used their instruments to ensure that we were level.

I lay on the deck of the helo, watching the heavy load sway beneath us, and called in the status to our pilots as they gained altitude, trying to avoid running into the side of the ship. I was prepared at any moment to release the load into the ocean and set our helo crash procedures in motion. Despite the fact that we were flying blind, we managed to remain calm, until suddenly the carrier deck appeared below us. I called in the altitude as we hovered and lowered the weapons to the deck. The load was gently released on the deck, and we landed safely, but it was a closer call than we would have liked.

The grim reality is that there are dangers in all of life, no matter the profession, but the stakes tend to be higher when you're talking about high-risk endeavors like military missions or high-altitude climbs.

In those intense situations, when lives are on the line, your mission is to enhance your skills to the elite level and prepare for every possible scenario that's within your control. And once you're confident you've done all you can, the only thing left to do is put your faith in God, believing that he'll deliver you from the things outside of your control.

•

On May 8, a Sunday, I called my mom.

"Happy Mother's Day!" I said.

"Oh, thank you!" I could hear the excitement rippling through her words. "I'm so glad you called." She hadn't been counting on a call from Everest base camp on Mother's Day.

"How is your climb going?" she asked.

"I went up to Camp III already, and now I'm just waiting for a weather window to make a summit attempt."

"Your dad and I are so proud of you," she said. I could tell she was crying. "You're in our prayers, and we love you."

"I love you too, Mom. Happy Mother's Day."

After I hung up, I sat there in silence for a moment, thanking God for my supportive family.

The day before we headed up for our summit attempt, we heard about an 82-year-old Nepalese man who had died in the icefall. Shailendra Kumar Upadhyay was trying to become the oldest man to summit Everest, but tragically, he didn't make it.

I was in my tent preparing my gear when I heard some commotion along the main path through camp. I unzipped the tent door and saw several Sherpas and Nepalese climbers with a body bag. They took turns carrying the climber's stiff body until they reached the helicopter pad, where they waited for the evacuation flight.

Nobody was sure of the exact cause of his death, but most people were leaning toward cardiac arrest. I could feel a sense of uneasiness settle over the group. *What was he like?* I wondered. *Did he have a family? Why was he climbing? What was his story?*

"Heavenly Father, please be with this man's family," I prayed. "I don't know much about him, but please comfort those who loved him. They must be dealing with great loss right now, and they need your strength to get through this."

On May 11 we decided to push all the way from base camp to Camp II in one day, and it would be a long one. The plan was to stay an extra day at Camp II, head up to Camp III, hit high camp, and then attempt the summit. If all went well, we'd return to Camp II after the summit and then go back to base camp the following day.

I gave JoAnna and the kids a call.

"I wanted to fill you in on the plans," I told JoAnna. "I'm

heading up tomorrow morning. We are hoping for a May 14 summit date."

"Really?" I could hear the slight trepidation in her voice. "How does the weather look?"

"We have a great window," I said. "And I promise I won't take any unnecessary risks. I'll be out of contact for a few days, but don't worry about me."

"Hi, Daddy!" Emily and Jordan yelled into the phone. "Thank you for the toys!"

I was glad they were enjoying their daily scavenger hunt. "Hi, guys! I miss you both so much. Are you being good and listening to Mommy?"

"Yeah," Jordan said. "Are you still climbing the tallest mountain?"

"Yep, I should be done in another week or so."

"How many sleeps is that?" Jordan asked.

"About seven to ten sleeps," I replied. "I'll have to see how the weather is."

All too soon, it was time for me to go. "I'll talk to you when I get down from the mountain," I said, my voice cracking. "I love you all so much!"

"I love you too, Daddy!" Emily and Jordan said in unison.

Then it was just JoAnna on the line. "So you'll be back down in five days?" she asked. "Will I hear anything before then?"

"I'll try to borrow a satellite phone up higher, but I can't promise anything," I said. "Keep up the prayers."

When I hung up, I buried my face in my hands and cried. *It's not like I think this will be the last time I talk to them,* I thought. *But there's so much unknown ahead.*

At around 4 o'clock in the morning on May 11, Bill and

I got ready in silence and then headed to the dining tent. Before leaving, I logged into Facebook and updated my status:

Heading to the summit of Mount Everest. BRB!

BRB—be right back. I certainly hoped it was true.

"How are you feeling?" I asked Bill over breakfast.

"Okay, but not perfect," he said. But he kept down his breakfast of instant coffee and oatmeal, so I took that as a good sign.

We put on our boots and jackets and then stepped out onto a thin layer of snow that had dusted the ground during the night. We lit our headlamps, donned our packs, and started out.

Bill and I carried our crampons and planned to put them on before we started climbing over the fallen seracs. As I walked through base camp, I slipped on the snowy rocks but quickly caught myself. I was grateful for the quick recovery; I would have hated to have to abort my summit attempt mere feet from my tent.

When we got to the edge of base camp, I looked over at Bill in time to see that he was vomiting again.

I was getting more concerned. "How are you doing?" I asked.

"I don't feel sick," Bill responded, wiping his mouth. "I just needed to throw up."

We put on our crampons and climbed through the icefall for the seventh time of our expedition. We agreed to go at our own pace and meet up at Camp II. Lakpa and Pasang would meet us there the following day since they wanted an additional day of rest down at base camp.

When I arrived at Camp I for a break, I sat in one of the shared tents we used for acclimatization, careful to not puncture the vestibule with my crampons. I opened a cattle feed bag, which the Sherpas had used to cache our food and supplies. To my surprise, the Sherpas had left a few Mars bars in the bag for me, and I stashed them in my pack for later use.

Then I decided to melt some snow for drinking water. It was difficult to keep the stove lit at such a high altitude with strong winds, so I had to use my body to protect the cooking area. I filled a cooking pot with snow and then placed it on the flame. Since snow is made mostly of air, it took several pots of snow to fill up my canister.

After getting enough water for Bill and me, I left Bill's portion in the pots. Then I wrote a note in the snow by the tent so he'd know where to find the water. I put my pack on again, reapplied sunscreen, and continued my journey toward Camp II.

When I approached the first major crevasse in the Western Cwm, I passed a man who was missing a leg and was wearing a modified crampon on his prosthetic foot. He was alone and moving slowly, but the look of determination on his face was unmistakable. I didn't know if he was going to Camp II or whether he planned to continue higher, but I was confident he'd reach his goal. I was inspired by his drive and his desire to overcome significant challenges. Even without a disability, climbing a mountain is a daunting task. I couldn't even imagine attempting it without the use of all of my limbs.

As he and I prepared to cross one of the ladders, we exchanged greetings.

"Beautiful morning!" I said.

"Yep." He didn't have much to say, and I could tell he was focused on the task at hand.

"See you up there," I said. "Be safe."

The sun was scorching, so I stripped down a few layers and applied additional sunscreen. At this point in the expedition, my skin was the darkest it had ever been, despite my constant reapplication of sunblock. At this high altitude, there were a lot more direct rays that came into contact with my skin. And since the sun reflected off of the snow and ice, it was easy to get burned in places that didn't usually see the sun—like the underside of my arms, the bottom and inside of my nose, and the inside of my ears.

In addition to the sunscreen, I wore a buff to protect my vulnerable face. The downside to the buff is that it filtered the air, and at that elevation, you need as much air as possible. I had little choice, however, because without it, the sunscreen wiped off every time my nose ran.

I was also careful to keep my goggles on. Not only did they protect my eyes from the blinding sun reflecting off the snow, but they also helped guard against UV rays. Since the atmosphere is thinner at higher elevations, it absorbs less ultraviolet radiation. In fact, ultraviolet radiation levels increase by 10 to 12 percent with every 3,000-foot increase in altitude.

In true Everest form, it went from being blazing hot one minute to whiteout blizzard conditions the next. Fortunately, another group that had gone before me had marked the route with wands, so I was able to find my way. Even though the snow was coming down in furious gusts, I was still hot from the penetrating sun. I continued to hike in a short-sleeved shirt, and I unzipped the side vents of my pants.

Halfway through the Western Cwm, I passed Dawa, our Camp II cook. He said Bill had radioed him, asking him to descend to Camp I to help carry his pack. Dawa was all smiles and offered me juice and chocolate. I thanked him but declined, since I still had my own arsenal of snacks and water.

I was less than a mile from our camp, which according to reports we'd heard from other climbers, had been destroyed days earlier due to high winds. Our Sherpa team had been able to salvage our tents and supplies, but it would take some time to rebuild camp.

By the time I arrived at Camp II, I was exhausted and eager for a break, so I went into the cooking tent to have a snack. After resting for a while, I walked out to where our tents lay collapsed in the snow. I put the tent poles together one at a time and stacked them on the canopy of the tent. I threaded each pole through, taking frequent breaks to make sure I didn't overexert myself.

I erected the tent, placed the protective fly over it, and anchored all the corners with deadman anchors. For the deadman anchors, I dug four holes, buried snow stakes in each, and then packed snow on top. This was critical for creating a firm hold when the snow froze.

Bill, Veronique, and her climbing Sherpas arrived an hour or so later, and we ate a lunch of hot soup, tea, and Spam sandwiches. The dining tent was a large eight-person tent with a couple of poles in the middle to keep it upright. The seats were made of flat rocks, which we lined with Therm-a-Rest pads for comfort. In the center of the tent there was a stack of rocks, which we used for a table, and the perimeter was lined with additional rocks for the stoves and our cooking supplies.

It had been a big day, so we took it easy the rest of the afternoon. Our personal tents had all been spared from the strong winds, but some of the shared tents were shredded, and our bathroom tent was gone. Thankfully, Dawa rebuilt it later in the day.

I post-holed over to my tent, creating fresh tracks in the deep snow. As soon as I unzipped the door flap, I fell onto the unrolled pad. With my feet still poking out of my vestibule, I removed my crampons and boots and then placed them inside, where I'd have easy access to them. Then, to ensure that no snow or ice would get inside, I stuffed my gaiters inside the boots.

After blowing up my air mattress, I set my −40-degree sleeping bag over the pad. As my last step in setting up house, I placed a picture of JoAnna and the kids in a transparent mesh pocket on the ceiling of the tent. As I lay on my make-shift bed staring up at their photo, I thought about how much I missed them. I knew it was impossible, but I wished they could experience some of this with me.

Our two rest days at Camp II were pretty low key, and we basically just went through our normal routine of relaxing in our tents and eating regularly scheduled meals. I also took advantage of the downtime to analyze my pack. I was using my heavy 95-cubic-liter pack, and I was concerned it would be too heavy at higher elevations. At such high altitudes, every ounce matters. I decided to do some investigative surgery, and when I opened up the lining of the pack, I found metal plates inside for back support. Since I would only be carrying a couple of oxygen bottles, I decided to remove the plates. I tried the pack on again, and I could tell a difference in the weight immediately. I only wished I'd thought of this weeks ago.

I spent most of my time in my tent listening to music, reading, and looking at pictures of my family. It seemed like an eternity ago that I'd been hugging them and listening to my kids' stories about their day at school. Now I was as far away as possible—on the other side of the earth, and higher up than most people could even imagine. Still, I was excited to finally be making my summit push.

As I thought through each scenario for the days ahead, the eagerness I felt was tinged with a sense of caution. I was about to climb into an unknown world, and I had no prior experience climbing above 23,000 feet. Those realities weighed on me. The only thing I could do was rest in the confidence that I'd prepared for this. I had to trust that my body would respond the way I hoped it would.

Back in AIRR training, the instructors' goal was to wreck us completely in simulation exercises so that the emergency situations themselves would seem easy by comparison. After doing full-body conditioning all morning until we could barely stand up, we'd head to the ocean or the pool for mile-long swims or other intense conditioning. Then we'd swim sprints and perform buddy tows, all while wearing full rescue gear (a harness packed with rescue devices such as knives, flares, and strobe lights), a rescue vest, fins, a mask, and a snorkel. We'd also have to tread water while holding bricks and simulate every worst-case scenario imaginable. Each day we asked ourselves why we were doing this, but after it was all over, we knew we'd be ready for anything.

•

On May 13 I awoke to hear Bill and Dawa talking in the cooking tent. I crawled out from the comfort of my warm sleeping bag and put on my layers, ready to climb to 23,700 feet. I deflated my air mattress and stuffed my sleeping bag into its compression sack. Then I checked my pack to ensure that there were no air pockets and that the weight distribution was balanced. If something was off kilter even a little bit, I would feel one side of my body aching partway through the climb.

When I walked into the cooking tent, I saw Bill hunched over on one of the rock slabs we used for seats. He informed me that he'd vomited during the night and still felt queasy. After a short discussion, we decided it was better for him to take an extra day at this altitude to let his body heal.

After breakfast, I headed up toward Camp III; Pasang would follow me up about an hour later. It was cold as I made my way through Camp II and onto the upper half of the Western Cwm. I pulled out my handheld video camera and recorded my ascent through camp. I couldn't stop smiling—and it wasn't just for the camera. I was finally making my way into position for a summit attempt! The reality was starting to hit me, and I couldn't hide my excitement.

I made it to the base of Lhotse Face relatively quickly and cached my trekking poles to the side of the main route. When I arrived at the bergschrund, I connected my safety devices to the fixed lines and started making my way up the ladder. A couple of Sherpas were coming down the ropes on the right side, so I connected to the left side, which was essentially a steep overhang of ice. It took a lot of effort to inch my way over the first obstacle, and I had to kick hard to gain solid purchase into the rock hard ice. Once I made it to the top, I rewarded myself with a quick rest and a drink of water, and then it was time to continue my steady pace toward my destination for the day.

When I first arrived at Camp III, I had no idea which tent was ours. Pasang told me it was on the opposite side of the fixed lines from where we'd camped on our previous acclimatization climb, but that didn't narrow it down much. I made my way around a couple of tents, being careful to remain clipped into the safety lines that wove around the icy ledge. A group of Sherpas was watching me, and I realized I must have looked hopelessly lost. *How does someone get lost at 23,000 feet in the air?* I wondered with a wry smile.

I finally came across a tent that looked similar to the ones we'd been using, so I unzipped it. To my surprise, I found some climbers I didn't know sleeping inside. Not wanting to feel like a burglar sneaking around in pure daylight, I decided to find a flat platform on the side of the icy face and wait for Pasang.

While I waited, I fumbled through my backpack, looking for some water. I glanced down just in time to see a lone Sherpa making his way up the mountain and figured it must be Pasang. Then I looked to my left and saw a pile of oxygen bottles, a bundled tent, and my ice axe. Sure enough, I was sitting on the platform where we would set up camp.

When Pasang reached my location, he sat down and took a brief rest before we worked as a team to erect our four-season tent. At this elevation, building a tent took a great deal of energy. Just putting the poles together required us to do pressure breathing, where you purse your lips and force the carbon monoxide out of your lungs to make them more ready for an exchange of oxygen.

Once the tent was built, we cooked dinner: tomato soup

and ramen noodles. We then watched as a group of guys attempted to ski down Lhotse Face. They appeared to be roped up, and they had their ski poles fitted with ice axe picks. They took the descent really slowly, knowing that one slip could result in an uncontrolled fall and almost certain death. Since the weather was fluctuating rapidly, they would ski for a bit, stop, and then start up again. It was taking them a long time to get anywhere, and I grew tired of lying there with my head poking out of the vestibule, so I burrowed into my sleeping bag and drifted off to sleep.

There's something about sleeping with oxygen that provokes extremely vivid dreams. All through the night I was transported to my childhood, reliving adventures and camping trips with my family. In one dream, I was in Mammoth, California, with my older brother, Rob, and my sister, Lisa, and we were all climbing rocks and fishing. I heard my dad playing "Barracuda" by Heart at an obnoxious volume, and I could even smell the clean scent of the pine forest. I was young and didn't have a care or worry in the world. Then I woke up and remembered where I was. I was climbing to the summit of Mount Everest!

The next morning we heard rumors about a Japanese man who had died near the South Summit. Although there were a lot of speculations, we weren't sure of the exact cause of death. As I always tried to do, I prayed for the victim's family—that they'd come to a place of understanding despite the pain. I didn't know this man's specific circumstances, but it was a sobering reminder about the need to be humble in the shadow of this mountain.

I never wanted to have a "summit or die" attitude; in the end, it's a mountain, and no mountain is worth dying for.

•

On May 14 we headed up to the South Col, where the highest camp in the world is located. We were entering the death zone. To get there, we had to climb straight up Lhotse Face for about a mile and then cut over at the Yellow Band, a section of layered marble, phyllite, and semischist that looks yellow against the stark whites and grays of the rest of the mountain. Then we had to traverse up and over the Geneva Spur—a rib of black rock that requires an angled climb.

The entire route was equipped with fixed lines, which made it safer but also meant that each step required significant effort, due to the constant steep angle of the climb. All your movements feel like they're in slow motion, and you have to preserve your energy as much as possible. I tried to find a steady pace and then stick with it. It's like running a marathon at that point—you don't worry about if other people are ahead of you or behind you; you just keep plodding along.

About 1,000 feet above Camp III, I stopped to get some water. I anchored myself to an ice screw with some cordelette and a carabiner attached to my harness. As soon as I set my anchor and tested its integrity, I pulled off my goggles, which I looped through my arm, and then removed my oxygen mask. Right at that moment, my crampon slipped on the unstable ice. To break my fall, I automatically reached for the fixed line with the hand that was holding my goggles. In a flash, my goggles slid off my arm and fell down the steep face. I watched in horror as my eye protection escaped into the abyss of ice.

It seemed the goggles were sliding down the mountain

in slow motion. And I didn't have a backup pair. If you're doing an intense climb like Everest, you simply don't have room in your pack to bring extras of anything—and whatever additional gear you take means extra weight you have to carry with you.

Down the mountain to the right, there was a vertical field of ice with several open crevasses, and my goggles were heading straight toward it. Then, miraculously, they curved back to the left and were stopped by the Sherpas going up the fixed line. I let out a breath, not even realizing I'd been holding it in.

A group of Sherpas who were heading up to Camp III grabbed the goggles. They motioned to me that they had them and that I could come down and get them. I was so relieved that they'd been able to stop them from descending farther, but that meant I'd have to retrace my steps and hike back down 500 feet. Still, it was worth it to have something to cover my vulnerable eyes.

Pasang was a little ahead of me, so I shouted up to him, "Pasang, I dropped my goggles. I'm going to rappel down to get them."

"That's not good," he said. "Be careful. I'll go to the South Col and make tents." Pasang continued his slow ascent up the hill.

I secured my pack, including my oxygen bottle and my mask, to the anchored ice screw, took a couple of breaths of oxygen, and rappelled down the face to retrieve the goggles. It was easy going down since gravity was on my side, but I knew going up would be more of a challenge. As I got close to the rope where the Sherpas had attached the goggles, I slowed down to make sure I didn't accidentally dislodge them from the fixed rope. When I reached out to untie the knot, I noticed that the goggles were cracked right through the middle of the inside lens. The outer lens was still intact, leaving only one layer for protection against ultraviolet rays. I didn't have too much time to think about the implications, though, so I put them on, connected my jumar and safety line, and headed back up without the use of supplemental oxygen. When I arrived at my backpack, I took a couple of hits of oxygen and then donned my full gear again.

At that moment I knew I was up against a challenge. The instant I turned on the regulator on my oxygen mask, my goggles fogged up. Goggles tend to get a little foggy at such low temperatures under normal circumstances, but usually you can use your gloves to scrape away the fog or ice. Now, with a crack through the center of the goggles, they were freezing between the layers. That meant I couldn't see out of them, and there was no way to clear them. I tried wearing my sunglasses instead, but with the oxygen mask strapped across my forehead, I couldn't keep the glasses close enough to my face to stay on. During the rest of my journey to the South Col, they were so iced over that I could only see through a dime-sized circle on the left side of my goggles. I focused all my attention on the fixed lines, knowing how critical each step was for my safety.

That morning almost everyone making a summit attempt turned around at the South Summit. When we passed one group on their way down, they stopped briefly to give us a report.

"It's too windy on the South Col," they said. "People's tents are being destroyed."

We'd heard that the winds were strong, but the predictions were for calmer conditions for the next day, and we hoped it would settle by the time we reached high camp. We decided to press on, using every ounce of stamina and mental focus we had to push against the 70-mile-per-hour winds.

At one point I saw a couple of Sherpas helping a man down the mountain. As they got close enough for me to see his face, I knew immediately what was wrong: he'd gone snow blind.

Snow blindness is damage to the cornea—usually temporary—that comes as a result of exposure to UV rays. In snowy conditions, the risk for this condition is higher, since the sun constantly reflects off the ice. On Everest there's even greater risk due to the extreme elevation and the lack of ozone protection.

How terrifying, I thought. It was challenging enough to come down the steep Lhotse Face with your vision intact; I couldn't imagine what it would be like to attempt it blind.

Pasang was pretty far ahead of me, but I was able to see his movements by periodically lifting my goggles to get a clearer view. At several points I saw him bend over, and other climbers went over to check on him. I wasn't sure what was going on, but he didn't look like his usual strong self. *I hope he's okay,* I thought, wishing I were closer so I could find out more information. I kept my pace of resting three to four seconds between each step. *Emily, Jordan, JoAnna.* Step. *Emily, Jordan, JoAnna.* Step.

Then all at once I heard a huge gust of wind above me. Instinctively I hunkered down to protect myself against whatever was coming over the rock band. Through my limited vision, I looked up to see a gust of spindrift (snow spray from high winds) kicking off above me near the Yellow Band. I was afraid that the extreme winds would push a loose snow slab down on top of me, but it blew right over before disintegrating into the wind.

With gusts like these, I had to be alert at all times. When I finally made it to the last traverse around the Geneva Spur, I heard a loud cracking sound—almost like a whip. I lifted my goggles in time to see a 100-mile-per-hour mini-tornado circling above me. I'd never witnessed anything like it before. It gained speed and hurled large rocks as if they were mere pebbles. I knelt down and grabbed the fixed line, ducking my head and preparing myself for a ride. But just as quickly as the twister had started, it was over.

I stood there in disbelief, trying to process what had just happened. At such high altitudes, with little to no protection, you simply can't predict what the weather will do. I had just witnessed a rare anomaly of nature—one that could have had disastrous consequences. I pulled my water bottle from my pack, unclipped my oxygen mask, and took two mouthfuls of water. Then I continued to make my way up.

As I climbed over the Geneva Spur, I tried to take in the views. I had heard it was a beautiful stretch of the journey, but it was difficult to see anything through my frozen goggles. Every once in a while I'd look under my goggles to get a glimpse of the mountainous grandeur surrounding me.

The summit of Everest is intimidating under any circumstances, but now, as I watched 70-mile-per-hour winds tearing up to the top, I could only stand there in awe.

I stopped to get a quick snack and some water, and then I took out my camera, managing to snap a few pictures before it froze and stopped working. I knew I just had to warm up the battery to revive it, but I decided to keep it stashed for now. These weren't exactly prime conditions for touristy photos.

The Geneva Spur arches in such a way that you can't see high camp until you're actually there. It was hard to keep putting one foot in front of the other without being able to tell if I was making progress or how much farther I had to go. Then all at once, I looked up and saw various tents and oxygen bottles scattered around the icy, rocky ground. I exhaled, my relief mixed with joy. *I made it to the highest camp in the world!*

With the combination of the rough weather conditions and the major elevation gain, from 23,000 feet to 26,000 feet, this climb to the South Col had been one of the hardest days of climbing so far.

But my adrenaline was pumping now. In five hours, we'd be attempting the summit.

I staggered around the windy camp, stumbling on rocks with my crampons, and wondering how I'd find Pasang. From a distance, I saw a Sherpa wearing a down suit that looked like Pasang's and made my way over to him.

"Hi, Pasang," I called.

But when he turned, I realized it wasn't him. The Sherpa pointed me in the other direction, indicating that I might find Pasang on the other side of camp.

I set out in search of a familiar face, and finally Pasang stuck his head out of a tent.

"Hi, Brian," he said.

"How are you feeling?" I asked.

He brushed my question aside, waving me into the tent.

We rested for a while, wearing oxygen at a low rate. The winds raged around us, and I was sure that the flimsy walls of our tent would be shredded at any moment. The wind gusts consistently hammered one side of the tent, compressing the poles, and the sound of the flapping fabric was deafening.

With the overwhelming sense that the walls were closing in around me, I was tempted to burst out of the tent and run to safety. *But where would I run?* I wondered. I had no choice but to sit there and pray that Mountain Hardwear had stitched each seam correctly.

I handed Pasang my goggles and showed him the crack that had appeared when they fell. The goggles still had a frozen layer between the lenses, so I decided to rip out the cracked layer. Both sides of the broken plastic came out clean, leaving a single layer. *Perfect!* I thought. *Now I'll be able to scrape them off, and I'll actually be able to see when I make my summit attempt.* There was only one problem—and a significant one, although I didn't realize it at the time: I had just cut my UV protection in half. And I'd done so in a place where the ultraviolet radiation is 100 percent higher than it is at sea level.

•

Pasang radioed base camp to check the weather forecast. Would we be able to make our summit attempt? After a few minutes, we received a Swedish forecast and a Seattle forecast about Everest's weather, which seemed to agree with each other. I had to smile at the thought that my home city was predicting the forecast for me now that I was halfway around the world. Twenty- to fifty-mile-per-hour winds were expected on the summit, there was no precipitation, and the temperatures were well within our range.

"What do you think?" Pasang asked me.

"Well, it sounds like we won't have any traffic jams," I said with a smile. You wouldn't expect a place like Everest to get congested, but with the fixed lines, you pretty much have to climb single file. And with a short climbing season and limited weather windows, there can be a lot of waiting time, which isn't good for the toes and fingers.

Pasang agreed and radioed down to the rest of our group that we were going to set out at 7 p.m. Bill was still a day behind, and he and Lakpa would move to high camp while we were heading for the summit. That meant we would be the only two people going for the summit, which is extremely rare. Some people (only a couple of whom were successful) had made attempts the day before during harsher winds, and several other climbers were waiting until the following day for calmer conditions.

Pasang and I were both feeling strong, so we figured we'd take off early, hit the summit, and return before the real winds started. And then if anything went wrong in between, we'd be able to turn back and still get to the South Col before conditions changed.

As I lay there on my sleeping bag that afternoon, I couldn't stop thinking, *I'm at the highest camp in the world!* Inside the bright orange walls of the tent, I could have been any place on earth. I'd been inside countless tents like this in the past. I'd smelled the same stale air mixed with low-flow oxygen. I'd heard the same whipping of wind outside. But this time it was different. This time it was Everest.

I stared up at the ceiling and watched the poles compress with each fierce gust. After a while, the wind started to calm down until it was merely a gentle breeze. Then it became silent, aside from our slow breathing behind oxygen masks.

Pasang was quieter than usual. I noticed that he didn't quite seem like himself, but I was in my own world, trying to take in this surreal situation. After all the training and preparation, I was about to get out of my tent at 26,000 feet and start walking toward the summit of Mount Everest!

Heavenly Father, I prayed silently, *please watch over us as we make this summit attempt. Please guide us and keep us safe. Thank you for your faithfulness and for everything you've provided for me. I'm grateful for the abilities you've given me, and I'm thankful to have this opportunity. Please take care of my family and give them peace. Amen.*

CHAPTER 7

SOLO ASCENT

LORD, you are my strength and my protection,
my safe place in times of trouble.

JEREMIAH 16:19, NCV

ON MAY 14, our summit attempt date, I didn't sleep a wink. We were scheduled to make the final climb later that evening, and although my main goal for the day was to take it easy, my body and my mind were whirling too rapidly for me to get much rest. After a dinner of soup and noodles, I lay on my sleeping bag, alone with my thoughts. *I'm only 3,000 feet and nine hours away from standing on the highest place on earth!* I could barely get my mind around the idea.

It was hard not to overthink things, but I tried to control my excitement so I could focus on each task at hand. Pasang and I geared up in silence, putting on our crampons and harnesses and checking our oxygen. The sun was just dipping below the mountains, and the moon was glowing silver on the horizon. The moon was almost full that evening, and the wind had died down significantly over the course of the day, so the conditions would be perfect for a night climb.

As I stood in the fading rays of sunlight on the South Col, I took some pictures to try to capture the moment.

The spell was broken when I heard the crackle of Pasang's radio.

"We're heading up the hill," he reported to the rest of our Sherpa crew down at lower camps. Our summit attempt was on!

Shortly after eight o'clock, we left the safety of our tents and made our way toward our ultimate destination. After crossing the quarter mile of the South Col, we began the steep mile that leads up to the Balcony, which at 27,500 feet is usually considered the halfway mark. Shortly after we started, I felt a dreaded pulsing in my head. *Oh no,* I thought. *Lord, please don't let this be an altitude problem. After all my preparation, I really wanted to reach the top.*

We took a moment to rest, and I told Pasang, "I'm afraid I have the beginnings of a headache."

"Headache is not good. Go back?"

I was surprised—it wasn't like him to want to turn back so quickly. "Let me get some water and a snack first."

I sat down and took out my thermos, and to my relief, the headache passed within a few minutes.

We made our way up the bulletproof ice and across a bumpy area called "the ice bulge." I noticed that my head-lamp was getting dim, even though I'd just replaced the bat-teries, so I swapped it out with a spare headlamp I'd brought along. Suddenly the path lit up before us.

That's about when my second wind kicked in. I started moving efficiently up the mountain, moving ahead of Pasang, who was carrying extra bottles of oxygen. I didn't know it at the time, but I later found out he vomited most of the way up. As I continued climbing, I noticed the way the moon reflected my shadow against the snow. My silhouette was with me the entire climb, keeping me company.

It's hard to explain, but even though I was climbing alone, I didn't feel alone. Researchers have studied this phenomenon, often called the "Third Man Factor," in which people in survival situations, such as climbing Everest, trekking through Antarctica, or sailing solo around the world, experience a presence by their side, helping them succeed. I'd never experienced anything similar before that night, but I was grateful to have the company. I didn't really take the time to analyze the phenomenon at the time, but looking back, I now realize how true it was—I really wasn't alone. God was present with me every step of the way. The Bible puts it this way: "The LORD himself goes before you and will be with you; he will never leave you nor forsake you" (Deuteronomy 31:8).

I hoped that whatever JoAnna was doing right now, she felt that same presence I did. Our faith in Christ was what kept us grounded—both when we were together, raising our kids and going about our daily lives, and when we were apart, facing the challenges that come with a lifestyle like mine.

I was raised Lutheran, and my family went to church every so often, but it wasn't much of a personal thing for me when I was growing up. JoAnna, on the other hand, was raised Southern Baptist, and she and her family sat in the front row every Sunday.

When I joined the military, my faith gradually became a central part of my life. It wasn't like I set out to become spiritual or anything, but at boot camp, you had the choice of working out on Sundays or escaping by attending church. There was never an empty pew. I don't remember the actual date, but a couple of years after boot camp, after hearing more about who God was at church and reading more about him in the Bible, I asked Jesus Christ into my heart.

JoAnna and I had been dating for almost a year at the time, and we had just gotten into an argument about something. I was really down and decided to go surfing by myself to clear my head. I paddled out into the ocean on my board and floated up and down with the current, waiting for a break to catch. As I sat there floating on my board at Sunset Cliffs, watching the gentle rise and fall of the tide, I wasn't praying or thinking about God, but out of nowhere, I felt a surge of life enter my body. I looked up as the clouds parted and fingers of light stretched toward the ocean waves, illuminating a pod of dolphins that were catching the surf. I sat there with an overwhelming sense of purpose.

"Jesus, I give myself to you," I prayed. "Please take control of my life. I want to live completely for you." It was a beautiful entry into the new me, and each day since, it has been a journey of getting to know God better. That day as I sat on the beach, I had no way of knowing that my journey would take me to the top of a mountain one day.

The route was a steep incline made of frozen snow, ice, and rock. I moved consistently, taking frequent rest steps and doing pressure breathing. The only sound I heard was my breath, flowing in and out through my oxygen mask. I started to see remnants of fixed lines from past years scattered on the path.

In the past, climbing expeditions regularly left gear and

supplies all over the mountain. The mentality was that if you didn't need it anymore, there was no reason to lug the extra weight with you. And at that altitude, most people are doing everything they can to survive, so cleaning up on the descent tends to be a low priority in the death zone.

But over the years, as more people have climbed Everest and there's growing awareness about caring for the environment, climbers tend to be more diligent about cleaning up after themselves. Plus, there have been a number of expeditions sent out in recent years with the sole purpose of cleaning up the gear from previous years. Even so, you can still find tattered tents, old anchors, fixed lines, dead bodies, and empty oxygen canisters strewn on the mountain.

I kept my focus and was diligent about staying attached to the rope at all times. I made sure to remain on the right lines—yellow with black stripes for this season. I trusted the Sherpas' diligence in anchoring the route, but each time I approached a new anchor, I still checked to make sure the anchor was fastened securely into the ice. Even if they'd been installed properly, anchors can wobble loose over time—either from overuse or from the sun melting the snow around the base. If they remain deep in the snow and ice, though, the freezing temps at night will solidify them for the next day's climbs.

Halfway to the Balcony, I had to negotiate up and around some rocky terrain. I kept looking back for Pasang, but he continued to get farther behind. I wasn't too concerned since it's common for climbers to get into different grooves, especially if you aren't roped to each other. I just figured he was moving at his own pace, so I decided to make my way to the flat Balcony and wait for him there. It was hard to tell in the darkness, but this last section seemed steeper than the rest of the route. I couldn't see how much farther I had to go, so I continued placing one foot in front of the other. That was the only way I would get there.

By the time I made it to the Balcony, I could barely see Pasang's headlamp down below. While I waited, I noticed some other headlamps heading up Lhotse directly across from me. *Are they looking this way?* I wondered. *Are they curious about whose single headlamp is moving up Everest?*

I also saw an electrical storm in the distance, which looked like an air bombing you might see footage of in a news report about a war-torn country. I took out my video camera and filmed the storm so I could research what I was seeing when I got home. Then I turned off the camera and just took in the moment. The silence was eerie, broken only by periodic wind gusts and my slow breaths through the oxygen mask.

Standing there at the Balcony, I couldn't help but think about Beck Weathers and his miraculous descent 15 years prior. Beck was a part of the 1996 tragedy that unfolded in Mount Everest's death zone. A previous eye surgery had made his eyes more sensitive, and he had lost his vision as a result of the high altitude and the exposure to ultraviolet radiation. He became blind at the very spot I was standing.

Beck's group, led by Rob Hall, had continued up toward the summit while he stayed behind and waited for their return. After an unexpected storm engulfed the mountain, eight people died. Rob Hall, a guide from New Zealand, could have made it down safely but opted to bivouac with another client, Doug Hansen, who ended up dying during the night. Rob perished 30 hours later, but before he passed away, he was patched through via radio and satellite phone to his pregnant wife back home to say some final words. His body still remains on the mountain, although it's out of view from the normal route. Rob's wife, Jan, said that's where he would have wanted to stay, so no one has tried to recover his body.

A couple of the other group members managed to make it back down to where Beck remained—suffering from frostbite and hypothermia, but still alive. They short roped him down to the South Col, but the whiteout conditions forced them to stop and hunker down for the night before they reached camp. The temperature dipped below −100 degrees Fahrenheit that night, and without protection against the elements, Beck went into a hypothermic coma. He was presumed dead and left behind. In the morning, a couple of Sherpas found Beck still breathing and put together a massive rescue to get him down the mountain. He ended up losing both hands and needing reconstructive surgery on his severely frostbitten nose. As remarkable as his story was, it wasn't one I was hoping to re-create.

It was pretty cold on the Balcony, so I kept pacing to stay warm. I was so tired that I could have closed my eyes and slept right there, but I knew that would be a recipe for disaster. Plus, it was so cold that my eyelids froze shut when I blinked, so I tried not to shut them any more than I had to. I was sure my eyelashes were being ripped off with each blink.

Finally, after about an hour of waiting, I saw Pasang making his way up to the Balcony.

"Do you have extra water?" Pasang asked. He took a swig of my water and immediately vomited.

Wiping his mouth, he said, "I don't feel good." He held out the water bottle.

"Keep it," I said. "Can you continue? Or do we need to head back down?" I'd never seen him ill before, and I was concerned.

"No, I'll be okay," he insisted. "Let's go."

We rested for a little while on the Balcony, and I was relieved to see that he managed to keep down a CLIF BAR. We both swapped out our oxygen bottles in preparation for the second half of the climb to the summit. I was still concerned about Pasang's condition, especially since we were alone on the mountain. But he assured me he wanted to keep climbing, so we headed up across the first ridge toward the South Rock Step.

After about 20 feet, my headlamp went dead. I knew that batteries burn more quickly in high altitudes and cold weather, but I couldn't believe it had happened already—I'd just put in new ones before our summit push. Changing the battery was no small task in the cold. I tried to pry open the battery area with my gloves on, but I wasn't able to get it. I had to expose my bare fingers to the air so I could wedge my fingernail into the slot. I put in the new batteries, and the headlamp came to life, lighting up the entire side of the mountain.

I reached into my down suit to put the old batteries into one of my pockets when Pasang asked for them. I dropped them in his open mitten, and he immediately turned and threw them off the side of the mountain. So much for leaving no trace behind!

We continued up the snowy ridge to almost 28,000 feet. The ridge was corniced over, and my crampons punched through in a couple of areas. I made sure to stay to the left side, which was more solid. Once we'd made our way across, Pasang put his hand on my arm.

"Brian, I'm too sick to continue," he said. "If I go with you, it will be danger for me."

I pulled up my oxygen mask so I could talk. "Do you need me to go down with you?"

"No, I'll wait for you at the Balcony." He gave me a serious look. "You summit alone."

He rummaged in his pack. "Here is the radio. And extra oxygen." Pasang placed the orange oxygen cylinder in the snow for me to retrieve on my descent.

I was disappointed that Pasang wouldn't be able to summit—both for his sake and for mine—but I knew he was making the smart decision based on his condition. You have to listen to your body as soon as you know you're not going to make it—the top of the mountain isn't the time to negotiate.

Now I had to make a decision: would I make the summit attempt solo? I had to weigh the risk versus the reward. This was a critical moment.

I had soloed plenty of other mountains in the past, so I wasn't worried from that perspective. But then again, this was Mount Everest. I ran through a mental checklist, trying to be logical and analytical about my decision. Other than being sleepy, I felt strong and didn't have any signs of acute mountain sickness. The weather was calm, and although I might face some wind gusts up higher, it didn't look like there would be anything worth turning back over. I didn't have any checks inside me indicating it would be unwise to continue on by myself.

The biggest question was whether Pasang could descend alone. If he needed help, there was no question about whether I would continue.

"Are you sure you can make it down alone?" I asked.

"Yes, I'm fine," he assured me again. I could tell he was a little worried to leave me alone, but he knew that I was capable. "You're a strong climber. You'll make it."

Then, before I could say anything else, he started descending.

I breathed a prayer as I continued up on my own: "Lord, go with me." I didn't look back.

•

This wasn't the first time I'd had to make a tough decision about whether I'd keep pressing on in the face of adversity. During my third week of AIRR training, I made a call home one evening to check in with my family. I knew something was wrong the moment I heard my mom's shaky voice.

She kept fumbling over her words like she had something to tell me, but she couldn't seem to choke it out. She knew how tough my training was and didn't want to upset me with bad news, but eventually I managed to get the truth out.

"It's your grandpa," she said. I was really close to my grandfather, and my stomach knotted, wondering what bad news she bore.

"He was diagnosed with cancer." She took a breath, and I could tell there was more. Apparently he'd seen how much my grandmother had suffered for two miserable years before the cancer took her life. He didn't want to endure all that himself, so he'd decided to end things quickly. One night, when he was at home alone, he'd stuck a pistol in his mouth and pulled the trigger.

My mom just happened to show up minutes later to find him on the floor drowning in his own blood. She called 911, and emergency responders came quickly and were able to revive him.

"The bullet missed his vital organs," she told me. I could hear the tears in her voice. "They transferred him to the hospital. He's on life support."

I faced a major decision in the middle of some of the toughest training the military has to offer. Would I go home to be with my family and see my grandfather? Or would I continue with my training?

Each morning the instructors lined us up in our freshly pressed uniforms for inspection and had us report about anything they needed to know.

The day after I heard the news about my grandpa, the question was the same as every morning: "Do you have any issues to inform us of?"

I stood silent.

I decided to compartmentalize this tragedy—and my emotions—and go on with my training.

I made it halfway through the week without telling anyone the news. I poured even more energy into my workouts and passed all the required physical training, but I ended up failing a simple academic exam covering helicopter search-and-rescue equipment. My mind was too distracted to focus on anything else.

One of the instructors screamed into my face, "How could you be so stupid? You'll never amount to anything."

I wanted to retaliate in anger, but instead I took a deep breath and shared about my grandpa's situation. Much to my surprise, he continued yelling at me for not telling him earlier.

But before I knew it, I was on an emergency flight home

to visit my grandpa in the Rogue Valley Medical Center. It was heartbreaking to see him lying helpless on the hospital bed, attached to tubes and surrounded by all sorts of beeping monitors. When I was a kid, I'd always thought of him as the strongest person in the world. He'd been a US Navy sailor during World War II and had manned the guns on the front of the ship. I grew up hearing stories about how he'd shot down enemy planes as they approached. He was a tough guy, but he had a soft side too, and when he came back from the war, he swept my grandma off her feet. Now, as he lay there looking like a shell of the man he'd once been, he told me something I'll never forget.

"I'm proud of you, Brian," he said. "I know your training is difficult, but do what you have to do, and be the best at what you do." It was the last time I saw him, but those words sank deep. I flew back to Pensacola with a renewed commitment to finish my training well. It's what Grandpa would have wanted.

And now, as I set off to finish my Everest climb solo, Grandpa's words echoed in my ears. I wanted to complete what I'd committed to, and I wanted to do it the very best I could.

Although summiting alone wasn't the scenario I'd planned out, I felt confident and comfortable as I set out solo around three o'clock in the morning. Back home I usually trained alone, so the motions felt familiar. When I wasn't thinking about being on Mount Everest, it seemed like I could have been on any of the Washington peaks near my home. And even more than before, I had the strong feeling that I was definitely not alone. That assurance gave me a sense of comfort, encouragement, and safety.

And in a way, the fixed lines up to the summit were a guide for me. I kept my grip on them, and they led me up the mountain one step at a time.

Without having to consider anyone else's schedule, I was able to move at my own comfortable pace. Just past 28,000 feet I reached the South Rock Step, which was strewn with fixed lines. I was surprised to discover how difficult this portion of the climb was. I hadn't read much about the area in my research since it tends to get overshadowed by the Hillary Step in books and movies.

I'd painted a mental picture of this spot based on the little I had read, but in this case the reality didn't look anything like what I'd imagined. The South Rock Step was a mid-fifth-class rock. I'd climbed rocks in tougher classes back home, but not at this altitude. If I'd been in Washington, a rock like this would be something I'd free-climb, with little or no protection. But above 28,000 feet, each step was an effort—and each rock scramble was triple the effort.

I wedged my crampon in the crack of a rock and then hoisted myself up with my jumar, which was attached to the fixed rope. Then I forced myself to rest for a moment, giving my heart rate a chance to return to normal. As I took three or four deep breaths, I looked up to negotiate my next move. I inched my way up the line, finding footholds to wedge my crampon points into and other areas to grip with my hands. The distance was short—only about 150 feet—but at a 60-degree angle and with the slippery rock conditions, I was surprised how quickly it drained my energy.

At about four-thirty in the morning, a halo of light hugged the horizon, indicating the sun was about to make its appearance. I was exactly where Pasang and I had planned we'd be at sunrise. Seeing the edge of sunlight gave me a new boost of energy. After a long night of climbing, this was a visible sign that I was making progress and nearing my goal. I paused for a moment to take it all in. Everest was casting its famous pyramid shadow over the Himalayas, and the valley was lighting up with a cascade of colors. I'd seen plenty of pictures of this scene, but none could come close to witnessing it firsthand.

I pulled out my video camera from one of my many pockets. I'd preset all the pockets with which items went where so I'd know exactly where everything was. This had saved me from a lot of fumbling around in the dark, trying to find sunblock, snacks, lip balm, and batteries. A familiar chime entered the air as I powered up the device, trying to capture this majestic moment. Seconds later the chime rang again, indicating that the camera had shut off. It had already frozen solid. It wouldn't be usable again until days later, when I would be able to let it thaw out and recharge on my laptop. I hoped I wouldn't lose the footage I'd gotten so far.

I put the video camera back into my pocket and continued my steady pace toward the South Summit, urged forward by the rising sun. The last snow hill leading up to the South Summit was fairly steep, and each step winded me. I was eager to reach the top, but I patiently took five seconds between each step. And then, finally, I breached the summit, where I sat to rest for a few minutes. As I paused to reflect on how far I'd come, my eyes started welling with tears, but I kept them in check. This wasn't the true summit—I still had another couple of hundred vertical feet to complete before I could truly celebrate. I pressed on.

I walked across a major ridge called the Cornice Traverse.

It's only a few feet wide, and according to Everest lore, it's a two-mile drop into Nepal on the left and a two-mile drop into Tibet on the right. It's always good to have options, I suppose. Earlier in the trip, one of the Sherpas had told me a story about his cousin, who had fallen off the cornice into Tibet a few years back.

I wonder what it would be like to fall that far, I thought. *Would you pass out and die before impact?*

I kept moving, taking small, careful steps and gripping the fixed rope tightly with my jumar. I made it safely past the exposed ridge and then looked to my left. I stopped in my tracks at the sight before me: unclaimed gear that had been recently abandoned.

Pasang and I had heard through the Sherpa grapevine that the Japanese climber Takashi Ozaki had passed away a couple of nights ago, and I figured this gear must have belonged to him. Takashi was legendary in the climbing world, having made the first full ascent of Everest's North Face. He'd also done winter climbs on six of the world's 8,000-meter peaks. But despite being in great shape, he'd started showing signs of pulmonary edema when nearing Everest's summit. He collapsed just a few hundred feet from the top and died later that afternoon.

They must have placed his body somewhere more discreet, I thought. But no one had taken care of his belongings. "Heavenly Father," I prayed, my heart heavy, "please bless this climber's family. And keep me in your care too."

It was eerie being the only person on the highest point in the world, thinking of all the other climbers who had died trying to reach this very location. And at that elevation, in the death zone, it's virtually impossible to carry the dead bodies down since you're using all the strength and energy you have to survive yourself. Since teams don't want to put their climbers at risk, they usually leave the bodies where they are or stash them behind surrounding rocks. At this altitude, it's too high for helicopter access, which means that many of the bodies of dead climbers remain frozen near the summit.

I later found out that Takashi had died below the South Summit, so it wasn't his gear after all—it must have been left behind by a previous expedition. But it remained a sobering reminder of the seriousness of what I was undertaking. I wasn't out of danger yet.

I reached inside my down suit and pulled out my camera. With the arctic temperatures and the fierce winds, I managed to get only one picture before it froze. I was able to put the camera back in my suit for a minute in between shots, allowing the battery to thaw enough to work temporarily. This was a time-consuming process, but eventually I was able to get a handful of pictures. As I snapped the panoramic view before me—Makalu, Lhotse, Kanchenjunga, Cho Oyu, and the other surrounding Himalayan peaks—I knew my camera would never capture the vastness of the scene. But I had to try.

The wind was picking up a bit as I reached the famous Hillary Step—a 40-foot rock climb and the last obstacle before I'd reach the true summit of Mount Everest. The Hillary Step got its name from Sir Edmund Hillary, the first person to successfully summit Mount Everest in 1953 with Tenzing Norgay. There weren't fixed lines then, so they had to free-climb up the rock obstacle. One wrong move, and they would have fallen for more than two miles to certain death.

At the Hillary Step, I saw dreadlocks of rope hanging all over from years of past climbing. On most of the route, the ropes were well tended by the Sherpas. But above the South Rock Step, there were ropes from the past several decades scattered around. Fortunately, though, the ropes for each year were color coded. I searched around until I found the yellow rope with black stripes and then connected my jumar and safety carabiner to the line.

The Hillary Step is one of the places that can get pretty congested since climbers have to go up one at a time and it can be a time-consuming process to traverse the Step. Since I was the only one summiting that day, I was fortunate to have no wait.

I climbed over the boulders and made my way to the left side, avoiding any potentially hazardous areas. As I was climbing up one of the sections, I saw that there was a deep hole between two boulders. *I wonder if there are any bodies stashed inside,* I couldn't help thinking. I forced myself not to look, deciding it was better not to know. Besides, I wanted to show respect to those who had passed away on the great mountain.

I inched my jumar up the thin lines and found placement for my crampons. Then I grabbed the rock with my free hand for balance. Perched high on the vertical rock face, I took a moment to pause and look out at the mountains. *I'm really here!* I thought. *I'm climbing the famous Hillary Step.* And then, as I made my way to the top, I saw my ultimate destination. The summit jutted out toward Tibet, with a windswept cornice at the top. It was plastered with prayer flags, white silk scarves, and a couple of bags containing extra fixed-line gear. I was temporarily paralyzed as I stood there, trying to take it all in. My eyes filled with tears, which quickly froze to my goggles. "Thank you, Lord," I whispered. I felt so much emotion welling up inside that I thought I might burst.

Then all at once I felt a rumble in my stomach alerting me that I had about a two-minute window before I needed to relieve myself. It had been a few days since I had gone, and the body's clock doesn't seem to operate based on the location of the most convenient restroom. It took me a while to shed my layers, and as I unzipped the back flap of my down suit, I had to laugh a little at the situation. *I'm at the summit of Mount Everest and about to add inches to its elevation,* I thought.

I tried to make it quick, as there were tender parts of my skin exposed to the freezing air. A gust of wind came as I was finishing, ripping the toilet paper from my hand and sending it sailing over the summit into China. *I guess I just did my business in Nepal and wiped in China,* I thought.

I pulled up my layers quickly to prevent frostbite. I'd have hated to explain that injury to people when I got home! I ran into trouble when I tried to zip my back flap, only to discover the zipper was frozen. No matter how hard I pulled, I couldn't get it to budge. By now my fingers were freezing in the elements. I alternated hands and kept working on the zipper until finally, after a few long minutes, it worked its way up.

I restrapped my back harness straps and took some deep pressure breaths, as the whole incident had taken a lot out of me. In keeping with my desire to leave no trace behind, I decided to kick my handiwork over the cliff into Nepal. Besides, I'm pretty sure future climbers didn't want that to show up in the background of their summit pictures.

As I approached the summit, the fixed lines turned into thin red ropes, which were tied together with fisherman knots. I had serious doubts that the lines would prevent a major fall, but I tried not to overthink it. Sometimes you just have to trust the equipment and lean on God for the rest. I slowly made my way across the final traverse, hunkering down every few seconds as strong gusts of wind threatened to knock me down.

And then it was the moment I'd been planning for, training for, dreaming about, and praying about for months—years, even. As I took my final step to the top, I saw my entire journey flash through my mind. All the climbs I'd made back home, before everyone else woke up. The countless conversations I'd had with JoAnna leading up to the decision to go. Saying good-bye to Emily and Jordan and then sitting on the stairs crying so hard it hurt. Watching JoAnna running through the airport to give me one last kiss before I departed. The weeks of travel to get to Nepal and then through countless villages on my way to Everest. Visiting the orphanage and giving gifts to the underserved children there. My headaches and swelling when I first arrived at base camp, leading me to wonder if I would even make it above 17,500 feet. The pivotal moment when I successfully climbed Island Peak. The many trips through the Khumbu Icefall, risking danger to create the blood cells I needed so I could make it at higher altitudes. The closeness with God I'd felt as I took in the striking views of the Himalayas. And of course the homesickness and isolation I'd endured as a result of being separated from my family for so long.

And then my crampon spikes pierced the windblown ice just below the bundle of prayer flags. I had soloed the summit of Mount Everest. I had the top of the world to myself! *At this moment I am physically higher than any person on earth.* I could hardly believe it was true.

"Thank you, Lord," I said, kneeling down. "Thank you." The tears flowed as a jumble of emotions coursed through my body. I felt everything from exhaustion to dehydration to pride to joy to gratitude to disbelief. *Is this really happening?* I wondered. In some ways the moment seemed utterly surreal.

And then, all too soon, it was time to think about turning back. I'd spent more than a month trying to reach this point, and now I could only stay for a short time.

I thought about the quote given to me by Chuck Thuot, an early climbing pioneer and a family friend. In his seven decades of life, Chuck has traveled all over the world and has climbed many impressive peaks, including Mount Logan (the highest peak in Canada), Denali, and Kilimanjaro, and he was one of the first people to climb Vinson Massif in Antarctica. He had his sights on Everest but was forced to reconsider when he was diagnosed with heart issues.

He had this quote by writer and poet René Daumal framed for me, and it perfectly captures the why of mountain climbing:

> You cannot stay on the summit forever; you have to come down again, so why bother in the first place? Just this: What is above knows what is below, but what is below does not know what is above. One climbs, one sees. One descends, one sees no longer, but one has seen. There is an art in conducting oneself in the lower region by the memory of what one saw higher up. When one can no longer see, one can at least still know.

The true summit is a small point that can fit only a few people. I'd heard that the north side, toward the Tibetan route, has a gorgeous view, but with the high winds and the 10,000-foot drop to the east, I decided not to risk peering over in that direction. I pulled out my camera and took a couple of self-portraits with the summit and prayer flags behind me. If I'd been up there with other people, we would have high fived, hugged, relived the highlights, and taken each other's pictures, but I was on my own. I savored my greatest mountain-climbing accomplishment alone, knowing I wasn't planning to return.

I had hoped to make a modified tripod so I could get banner pictures for my sponsors, but it was too cold and windy. I figured my sponsors would rather have me return in one piece than have a great photo anyway.

I sat down to gain my composure so I could make a radio call to the rest of the group. I was so choked up that I had to make a couple of run-throughs with the radio off. I didn't want them to hear my voice cracking. After three practice runs, I came off my oxygen and placed the call: "Calling all camps, this is Brian, checking in from the summit of Mount Everest!"

Almost immediately, I heard a roar of congratulatory remarks from all the camps manned by our Sherpa crew. Once the cheering died down, Bill came through from Camp III. He was excited to hear that his company had successfully put a person on the summit of the highest mountain on earth. And he was also happy for me.

"Congratulations, Brian!" he said. "Enjoy the top, and be sure that you and Pasang give us a radio call once you make it down from the South Summit."

That's right, I thought. *No one knows I'm alone up here!*

"Sounds good," I responded. "But Pasang felt sick and went back down a few hours ago."

Bill took a moment to absorb that information and then came back on the radio. "Okay," he said. "Be safe, and call us on the way down. Over."

"Roger that!" I replied. Then I turned down the volume a bit.

What I didn't realize until later was that I'd turned not the volume knob but rather the digital frequency knob. That changed the preset channel I was using.

After the radio call, Bill asked Lakpa, one of the climbing Sherpas, how long it would take someone like me to descend from the summit.

"Someone like Brian?" Lakpa said. "Two to three hours."

They didn't hear from me again for seven hours.

CHAPTER 8

DESCENDING ON FAITH

Let us, then, feel very sure that we can come before God's throne where there is grace. There we can receive mercy and grace to help us when we need it.

HEBREWS 4:16, NCV

I STOWED the radio in the outside pocket of my pack to ensure that it was secure. Then I put my mask back on and sucked in a couple of long breaths of oxygen.

The morning sun was moving higher in the sky, so I put on my goggles. As soon as I did, however, they fogged up and froze. I tried wearing my sunglasses, but the oxygen mask kept getting in the way. My mask covered only my nose and mouth, but the straps reached all the way around my head and cinched tight in the back. When I tried to wear my sunglasses over the mask, the straps pushed the sunglasses away from my face, leaving me unprotected against side sun exposure. Then I tried putting the sunglasses under the straps, but that caused the straps to dig painfully into my face.

I decided I'd just have to deal with frozen goggles.

It had been about an hour since I'd left the South Summit, so I figured it was time to start heading down. *It's hard to believe how much time I spent preparing for this,* I thought, *and now it's already over.* But I knew that for the sake of safety, I didn't have the luxury of basking in the accomplishment much longer.

I checked my gear to make sure I was ready for the descent and took a few final pictures from the summit. I looked up, and all at once, my vision got extremely blurry. With my light-blue eyes, I tend to be sensitive to sunlight, but this was unlike anything I'd experienced. Even when I was looking down, it felt like I was staring directly into the sun. Then suddenly, without warning, I couldn't see anything.

I knew immediately what was happening.

I was snow blind!

Snow blindness, also called photokeratitis, is essentially when the cornea of the eye gets sunburned. It usually isn't noticeable until hours after exposure, which means the damage had probably started the day before, when I was climbing up Lhotse Face. I was wearing goggles with compromised UV protection at an altitude where there's a 100 percent ozone risk. My eyes hadn't stood a chance.

Okay, I told myself. *Stay calm.* Facing the path toward the Hillary Step, I knelt down, felt around for the fixed line, and grabbed it with both hands. Everything around me was bright white, and I couldn't even see my hand in front of my face. If I squinted really hard, I could make out a few blurry objects up close, but I couldn't see anything in the distance.

I scrunched my eyes tightly, trying to get my bearings to make sure I didn't step off a cliff and plummet to my death. My heart was racing, but I knew I needed to control my body's natural response of panic and shock.

Fortunately I'd had my share of experience with keeping panic at bay in emergency situations. In AIRR training we spent time learning multiple-survivor rescues. We'd sit in the doorway of the simulated helicopter 10 feet above the water and assess the situation. After ensuring that the area was clear of debris, we'd jump into the pool, which was churning with rotor wash. Our mission was to rescue multiple victims— some of whom had parachutes draped over their helmets and were face down in the water, and others who were thrashing around in a panicked frenzy, trying to take us down as soon as we breached the surface.

From the moment we hit the water, the air pressure from the powerful rotor blades caused the water to spray out from the center of the helicopter. The force was so great that it felt like handfuls of gravel were being thrown in my face. With limited vision, I had to carry a 200-pound survivor into the mini-hurricane so I could find a rescue hook. Once I gained control, I'd call for the hoist operator to lift the survivor 80 feet to the helo.

After the panicked person was safely in the helicopter, it was time to assess the other survivors and stabilize them. I had to keep each survivor "in close and in control" while I went underwater, crawling down his spine to remove all the tangled parachute lines, also known as shroud lines. Because it's impossible to see anything in the darkness underwater, I had to navigate by touch alone. If I made a single mistake in a procedure, the survivor would become active, spinning around and latching on to me for flotation, which would take both of us under and put us at risk of drowning. In those critical moments, I had to stay calm and not panic.

Now, high on Everest instead of underwater, I took a few

breaths and tried to assess the situation. Reality quickly set in. *I'm at the highest point on earth, with no one else on the mountain,* I thought. *I'm going to have to descend on my own—without my vision.*

There was absolutely no chance of being rescued at that altitude. Nobody else was making a summit attempt that day, and the other groups had either already descended or were getting in position to make an attempt later that night. I'd heard of a few rare solo summits in the past, but even in those situations, there are typically other people on the mountain making attempts at the same time. *I'm truly alone on the summit,* I thought. *I'm above the death zone and truly alone.*

My radio was of no use since I'd scrambled the frequency earlier when I'd tried to turn down the volume. Even if it had worked, the mountain blocks radio transmissions from the South Summit down to the Balcony, so chances were I wouldn't have been able to make contact anyway. Besides, I never would have asked for help if it meant other people would have to risk their lives to try to save me. Rescue attempts at this altitude were nearly impossible—and it wasn't like there were groups sitting around at the South Col waiting to rescue struggling climbers. In mountaineering, you have to calculate the risks and then accept them if things go sideways.

I figured that Lakpa and Bill wouldn't miss me for another three hours. If I was going to survive, it would be entirely up to me. But I knew I wasn't really alone.

"Lord," I prayed, "please keep me calm and give me the strength to get down this mountain."

I inhaled deeply, held my breath for a couple of seconds, and exhaled. Then I stood up and began making my way down, using the fixed ropes hand over hand. Everything was a whiteout blur, but I still strained to see what little I could, knowing how dangerous a single misstep could be. I kept my hand gripped around my safety line and made sure both feet were firmly planted in the snowy ground.

My first challenge was the Hillary Step—an obstacle that some people deemed impossible to climb with vision. It helped that the rock was dark in contrast to the bright snow, but I had absolutely no depth perception. I used my sense of touch to maneuver in and out of the fixed rope through the various anchor points. With every changeover, I checked to make sure my carabiners were locked and the rope was properly inserted. With all the adrenaline coursing through my body, I felt utterly parched, but I was in no position to get my thermos.

Then it was time for the inevitable: I had to slowly lower myself down the step. Anchored to a section at the top, I went down the rock pendulum style. Although I couldn't see anything below me, I knew there was a 10,000-foot drop on each side of me and 40 feet of exposure directly below me. I had no choice but to trust my gear and proceed with caution.

Every move I made was ultraslow, as I had to be extremely cautious about each foothold and handhold. Then, about halfway down, my crampons slipped against the smooth rock surface, leaving me swinging sideways and slamming helplessly into the wall of rock and ice. Unable to even brace myself for impact, I let out a cry of pain. No one could hear me.

Maybe it will be easier to face forward instead of backward, I thought. I turned around so my back was against the icy wall, and I leaped to a lower boulder. I stopped my back-swing with my left arm. My heart was beating wildly, and my carotid artery felt like it was ready to burst out of my neck. I hunkered down on a flat snow shelf, trying to calm my body's systems. Finally, after a few minutes of deep, controlled breaths, my heart rate went down.

I fumbled through my pack to get some much-needed water. I removed my mask and cautiously unscrewed my thermos, careful to not drop the lid. I felt instant relief as the water made its way past my dry lips and down my throat. It had taken me more than 30 minutes to climb less than 100 feet. It was going to be a long descent.

The next section was the Cornice Traverse, which was a small pathway with two miles of exposure on each side. I gripped my safety line and took half steps, being careful not to let the spikes of my crampons snag the boot in front. I knew from memory what was on each side of me, but with no visual points of reference, I felt a nearly disabling sense of vertigo.

Keep your fear and panic in check! I coached myself sternly. These reactions are normal survival mechanisms, but with a long-term challenge like this one, I knew I'd need to rein in my emotions if I was going to survive. With my heart racing and my nerves tingling, I forced myself to focus on each step and not think about the enormity of the danger I was in.

Yet somehow I didn't feel alone, even as I made my way through this terrifying leg of the journey. In the Bible it says that faith is believing what we can't see, and in that moment, I experienced that truth in a very real way.

I thought about JoAnna and the kids back home. The mental image of them brought me a sense of peace as I focused on breathing and slowing my heart rate. *Emily, Jordan, JoAnna.* Step. *Emily, Jordan, JoAnna.* Step.

As I made my way down, the wind started picking up. Fifty-mile-per-hour gusts were blowing against me, so I hunched down to create a lower center of gravity. The gusts seemed to come in two-minute intervals, and the spindrift intensified. *This must mean the higher gusts are on the way,* I thought, remembering the mini-tornado I'd experienced near the Geneva Spur on the way up. I considered getting on my hands and knees and crawling across this section, but I figured I'd be better off anchored to the ground, with my spikes in the snow. I didn't want to find myself slipping off the side or through the cornice.

Some people have the idea that climbing is glamorous, but even under the best circumstances, there's nothing elegant about it. And as I made my way across the obstacles without the luxury of my eyesight, I could only imagine how awkward I looked. I inched my way across the traverse, taking small steps and bending down every so often, squinting my eyes so I could get a blurry image of where my feet were planted. I knew this wasn't speeding things along, but it helped me mentally to know that my feet were firmly planted on the ground.

Finally, after forcing myself to move one foot after the other, step after step, I felt the ground sloping downward, and I knew I'd made it to the edge of the traverse. I was on top of the ridge, heading to the South Summit.

I stepped off the traverse, my spikes digging into the warming snow. Wedging my fingers tightly into the carabiner, I sank backward and gently fell onto the top of the hill. I got up and took a couple of heavy steps, being careful not to snag the other boot.

I made it across the South Summit ridge and then stood

for a moment, trying to decide how to go about my next descent. If I'd had the use of my eyes, these areas would have been quick rappels for me. But now each descent was agonizingly long—not to mention exhausting. I did some quick calculations and realized I'd been climbing nonstop for more than 26 hours. I shut my eyes for a second to rest and felt myself doze off in an instant. I jerked my eyes open, and my heart started racing. *Wake up!* I berated myself. *If you fall asleep, you'll die!*

I stopped to get another drink from the large thermos in my backpack. I anchored off to an ice screw, took off my pack, and removed my oxygen mask so I could get a couple of sips of water. Then I put everything back on again. I hung my head, exhausted.

The more I thought about the gravity of my circumstances, the faster my heart rate became and the more oxygen I needed to breathe. *You need to focus,* I told myself. *Breathe in; breathe out.* I exhaled slowly, turning my mind to the next task at hand: strapping my mask back on.

•

Meanwhile, Bill and Lakpa were heading up toward the South Col, some 3,000 feet below—about five or six hours, under normal conditions. They tried making radio checks every 15 to 30 minutes, and after getting no response, they started to worry.

During a water break near the South Summit, I'd pulled the radio out of my pack and tried to place a call, but all I got was static. I held the radio a couple of inches from my face and squinted to try to make out the correct knobs, but I wasn't able to read anything. After a while, I decided my time would be better spent trying to get down the mountain. I placed the radio in my pack and didn't pull it out again.

I continued down from the South Summit to the place where I'd made a video of the sunrise on my ascent. It was hard to believe that just a few hours earlier I'd set eyes on this breathtaking sight, and now I couldn't see a thing. *That's mountain climbing for you,* I thought wryly. *You can take a turn for the worse in the blink of an eye.*

I had originally planned to grab a couple of rocks from the summit for my kids, but now that was the last thing on my mind. I just wanted to make sure their dad returned to them—and not in a body bag.

I kept heading down until I reached the top of the South Rock Step. At this point I faced a critical decision: should I rappel down the South Rock Step as I would have normally, or should I swing the rope to the left side, down a steep wall of snow and ice?

Rappelling with crampons on a rock face requires precise movements and a great deal of focus. With their steel spikes, crampons are made to pierce ice and snow, not rock. If you don't wedge a spike into a rock crack properly, you risk slipping off the granite surface. *Can I do that based solely on feel?* I wondered.

I decided to go down the left side to descend the snowy 70-degree slope. As I contorted my right foot to gain purchase on the steep slope, I suddenly felt a pop as my crampon released from my boot. As if in slow motion, the dark, blurry object toppled down about 20 feet and then stopped on the slope. I wasn't entirely sure the object below was my crampon, but I had to retrieve it. I couldn't get down without both crampons—not in these conditions.

"Lord, help me get through this," I prayed. "Please protect me."

Trying to remain calm, I took my first step, digging the spikes in my left heel into the thawing snow. I took my next step with the boot that didn't have a crampon, and as I dug my heel into the ledge, the snow gave way. Unable to break my fall, I tumbled head over heels down the steep slope.

My down suit could only do so much to cushion my flailing body as I bumped down the hill, ice jutting into my side, my back, my shoulder, and my head. I felt my oxygen tank digging into my back as I tumbled. My camera, which I'd tucked into my down suit, was crushing my ribs.

As I turned upside down, my tank slid from my pack but caught on the breathing tube, preventing it from falling thousands of feet down the mountain. Then I felt a major jolt as my safety-rope shock loaded. The weight of my entire body was caught by the extended rope, giving me the worst whiplash I'd ever experienced. My back arched, and my legs and arms bent backward, facing down the mountain. But I was alive. My safety harness and the fixed lines had just saved my life.

I lay there breathing hard, trying to recover from the shock. I'd just fallen down the South Summit of Mount Everest—blind. And so far at least, I was still breathing to tell about it.

My feet were above my head, but I didn't want to right myself because I was afraid that would cause my oxygen tank to fall out of my pack. Fortunately, I was still getting some supplemental oxygen, even though my mask had been ripped sideways, away from my face. I lay there forcing myself to remain calm and lower my heart rate.

Once again I was reminded of AIRR school. During training, the instructors would have us swim underwater for the length of a swimming pool and then swim freestyle back—and we had to repeat this over and over again, until we almost passed out. If we surfaced from an underwater swim early, the instructors would scream, "Control your breathing!" I'll never forget seeing one candidate who surfaced for air during a 25-meter underwater swim and then dipped back into the water, struggling to reach the other side without resurfacing. Breathless and oxygen deprived, he knew it would be better to black out and potentially drown than show the instructors he wasn't giving it everything he had.

As I carefully righted myself, I felt a presence telling me that I needed to get some water. I didn't hear anything audible, but the words *You should take a drink* filled my mind. I remember feeling surprised, and I said out loud, "That's a good idea!"

I couldn't escape the continued sense that somebody was there with me. I can't exactly explain it, but it seemed like there was a guiding presence by my side, leading me toward safety. In the moment, I didn't have time to analyze it, but in retrospect, I have no doubt that the Holy Spirit was with me. I'd never had such a tangible experience of the reality described in Isaiah 30:21: "Whether you turn to the right or to the left, your ears will hear a voice behind you, saying, 'This is the way; walk in it.'"

I hadn't been conscious of it, but I was completely dehydrated. To my knowledge, my mouth had never been so dry before, and the water revived me—in body and in mind. After drinking a few sips from my thermos, I squinted my eyes, searching for my crampon. It wasn't long before I realized the effort was hopeless. I'd probably fallen past it already, and even if I hadn't, the chances were slim that I'd ever see it unless I stepped directly on it.

I strained painfully through my scratchy eyes, desperately hoping to see something dark against the white canvas, but the bright light of the sun banking off the snow burned my eyes. Then all at once I looked above me and spotted a dark, blurry object.

"Lord," I prayed, "please let that be my crampon, not a rock."

I donned my gear and faced the daunting prospect of climbing up to check it out. I punched the toes of my boots into the snow a few times with each step to make sure I had full purchase. After placing my foot down each time, I took three long breaths and then used the safety line to pull myself up.

While still gripping the rope, I approached the object and reached down to feel it. Through my thick climbing gloves, I felt something sharp. I held the object close to my face. Sure enough, it was an even row of steel spikes!

"Thank you, Lord!"

Double-wrapping the rope around my arm, I stomped out a small one-by-two-foot platform to stand on as I put my gear back on. I took extra care tightening both crampons and weaving in the extra webbing of the straps to ensure I didn't trip on it. Then I slowly started traversing back to the safer rocks.

Not far from my platform, as I sidestepped toward Nepal, the earth below me broke loose into a small slab avalanche—the shifting that occurs when a block of snow breaks loose from a fracture and slides over the layer below. I immediately dropped into a self-arrest position, with the fixed rope in hand. Self-arrest—a method used to stop a fall—is typically done with an ice axe in hand, not a fixed rope. The idea is to roll and drive your ice axe into the snow while kicking the front points of your crampons. I didn't have my ice axe above Camp III, but after years of training, it was automatic to assume the position.

I rode out the fall in a glissade style—squatting and sliding down in a crouched position—all the while grasping the line as tightly as I could. I was going down so fast that the rope burned a line in my thick leather glove. I felt the sting of the friction burn and screamed out in pain, but at least I managed to stop my fall.

I lay sideways in the snow, again focusing on reducing my oxygen intake and rapid heartbeat. Even with the arctic temperatures, I was sweating profusely inside my down suit. I couldn't believe how much more exertion everything took now that I was short one of my senses.

The fall put me down lower on the South Rock Step, but I still had to get beyond the slippery slope. Although the granite surface was a blur, I was able to distinguish it from the snow. As I slid my hand down the fixed line, I reached an anchor and took a quick rest before connecting again.

I sensed the voice telling me again, *Brian, you should get some water.* I went through the process of removing my pack, coming off oxygen, and getting out my thermos. Then, out of nowhere, a stroke of genius hit. *Why not put your thermos in the inside pocket of your down suit?* Of course! It would optimize the process of getting a drink, and it would require much less energy each time.

I connected my jumar to the fixed line above the anchor, dropped my safety on the rope below, detached my jumar, and headed down the rock wall. The whole way, I held on to the rope with the fingers of one hand wedged into the carabiner and my other hand either on a rock or on the rope. I had to make sure that I had three points of contact on the ground at all times and that my crampon points stuck into cracks and flat areas of the rock. Easier said than done. Usually I blindly slid my spikes down the surface of the rock until they caught. In some cases they never caught, so I pulled myself back up and had to find another route down.

It was an agonizing process, and with each step, my mouth grew more and more parched. I had to stop often to quench my thirst, and I was grateful that my thermos was more accessible now.

The last section of the South Rock Step left me with a choice: I could do a large jump-type rappel, or I could do a sideways traverse. Both options had drawbacks. If I rappelled down, I risked falling straight down. If I went sideways, there was the potential that I'd pendulum back and smash into the rock surface. I decided to climb sideways, since a direct fall could result in broken bones, whereas swinging back might result merely in massive road rash.

I moved slowly to the side, basically hugging the rock to control my descent. Normally I would have been worried about ripping my expensive clothing, but at that point I didn't care one bit if my suit was shredded by the time I finished. I made it across safely and rewarded myself with a swig of water.

I had descended about 1,000 feet from the summit by this point, which felt like a significant accomplishment. But it was concerning, too, because that meant I was only one-third of the way to high camp.

On the little ledge below the South Rock Step, I tried checking my oxygen regulator. I brought the device about an inch from my right eye and tried to focus. From what I could tell, it seemed like I had about 5 percent left, but I couldn't be sure. All I knew was that the oxygen wouldn't last long, and I'd need to swap out my tank as soon as I reached the canister Pasang had left at his turnaround point.

As I started down a snowy ridge, the exhaustion of having climbed for almost 28 hours straight hit me. I was completely drained of energy, and I desperately wanted to sleep. It took a lot more energy than I could have imagined to do this without my sense of sight, but I kept forcing myself down the mountain. I walked with tiny steps and relied on the fixed lines, hand over hand.

Eventually I reached a familiar location: the platform where Pasang had turned back. I actually might have passed right by the spot, but thankfully the blurry bright orange object sticking out of the snow caught my attention. The spare oxygen bottle!

The platform area wasn't much bigger than a kitchen table. I remained attached to the fixed lines but dropped my pack so I could swap out the oxygen bottles. I popped off my face mask, since it would cause suffocation when I disconnected the regulator. For a moment the reality of my situation hit me: I was at 28,000 feet, off oxygen, unable to see, and faced with the prospect of making it to the South Col on my own.

I detached the old bottle but kept it in my pack so I wouldn't leave trash behind. Then I ran my gloved fingers over the top of the new bottle and screwed on the connector.

I brought the regulator inches from my face, hoping to see the blurry black indicator line all the way to the right, which meant full. From what I could tell, though, the line was pointing to the left. I decided to put the mask on to test it. I breathed in, and there was absolutely no flow of oxygen. I ripped the mask from my face.

Okay, let's figure this out, I thought. I disconnected the tube and cleared the ice away from the bottle. Then I reconnected again, but still no success. My mind raced. I knew I didn't have enough oxygen in my old tank to make it down. I felt panic setting in. *Breathe,* I coached myself for the 100th time that day.

I could see only one option: I'd have to make do with the current bottle and get as far as possible, then go without supplemental air. I reconnected the original bottle and took in some much-needed oxygen. *Well, you can't sit there and troubleshoot all day,* I told myself. I placed the other bottle in my pack and set out again. The extra bottle added 15 pounds to my pack, but it was ingrained in me not to leave trash on the mountain, so I headed down with less oxygen and more weight.

For the next part of the route, I had to cross the snowy ridge—the one I'd punched my feet through the night before. I moved with great caution, hugging the right side. As the day wore on and the sun grew brighter, the pain in my eyes became almost unbearable. It felt like rocks were scratching the inside of my eyelids, and no matter how hard I fought to keep them open, they threatened to shut of their own volition. My feet were heavy and clumsy, my legs felt like dead weight attached to my crampons, and my throat was constantly parched. I kept swiveling my head and squinting, trying unsuccessfully to find any blurry landmarks that would help me estimate my location.

At one point, at the height of frustration, I stopped, held the rope tightly, and yelled, "I will not die on this mountain!"

I felt tears welling up involuntarily. "Stay strong!" I coached myself. "Push forward—you will survive!"

I kept moving. The path started to open up a bit, and I approached a large, blurry rock formation. I recognized the flat area and position of the rope anchors. I was at the Balcony—halfway back to the South Col! *You've made it this far,* I told myself. *You're going to survive.*

When we'd made our original plan, Pasang had said he would wait for me at the Balcony. But since I was much later than planned, and the wind was picking up on the unprotected Balcony, I figured he must have decided it would be safer for him to head back to the South Col. I'd keep making my way down solo.

I sat down on a flat rock, closed my eyes, and felt myself drifting off to sleep, so I quickly stood up. I ate a handful of trail mix and drank some water. I wondered what everyone below was thinking by now. I wasn't sure what time it was, but I knew I'd been on the mountain a lot longer than planned. I had renewed energy, though. *I will not become another Everest statistic!* I knew there were more than 100 bodies still high on the mountain from failed summit attempts. Maybe that was the one advantage of my blindness: I wouldn't be able to see them even if they were mere feet away from me.

Before I headed out again, I took a moment to pray. "Heavenly Father, thank you for bringing me this far. I know you're with me, and I believe you'll get me to safety. Please, Lord, watch over my family, and help them not to worry."

I wondered what JoAnna and the kids were doing at that moment. I knew JoAnna was at a scrapbooking retreat that weekend and was probably starting to wonder how I was doing, since she knew I'd be attempting the summit that day. I thought about Emily and Jordan, who were probably sleeping, without a worry in the world.

JoAnna and I had met 16 years ago—in a hot tub, of all places. We both lived in the same apartment complex, and one night she and her friends happened to be in the complex's hot tub at the same time I was. She was so intimidatingly beautiful that I couldn't even look at her without becoming paralyzed with inadequacy.

I was 21 years old at the time and in the Navy, having just returned from a tour in the Persian Gulf. She was 20 and getting her psychology degree from San Diego State University.

"What do you do for a living?" one of her friends asked me.

Wanting to impress her with my quick wit, I said, "I'm a plumber." Then I stood up from the water with my plumber's crack showing.

Everyone laughed, but JoAnna thought I was a jerk.

But over time, it became clear that God had placed us in that pit of boiling water at the same time for a reason, and she eventually became interested in that jerk. We started going to a small church, Zion Avenue Baptist, together. We were young and had a lot of growing up to do, but our little church was a constant in our life, and it helped give us a solid foundation for our relationship.

JoAnna is deathly scared of heights—we couldn't be more opposite in that way. On her 25th birthday, I wanted to do something she'd never forget, so I took her up in a hot air balloon. She was terrified at first, but as dusk fell, we stood together watching the sun set over the ocean. Then she turned around to see me pull out a diamond ring. Between the flame bursts that kept us in the air, I said, "JoAnna, I love you, and I want to be with you forever. Will you marry me?"

I expected her to burst into tears of joy, but instead she started laughing. Then she said yes and threw her arms around me. After that she was so preoccupied with her excitement that she didn't even think about her fear of heights.

Did I make a mistake by deciding to attempt this? It was the first time I'd really started to second-guess my decision. But even as I stood at one of the highest points in the world, snow blind, alone, and exhausted, I knew I would never have been content with a lifestyle of sitting on the couch or squelching my ambitious goals. I believed that life was for living. I didn't want to take unnecessary risks, but I wanted to embrace the big dreams that burned inside me. I also wanted to be a role model for my kids about what it looks like to accomplish what you set out to do.

My desire was to live life to the fullest and have no regrets. If the doctor gave me bad news one day, I wanted to be able to say I'd lived a full life and would do it all over again if I could. I hoped to live each day knowing that I was making the most of it and being faithful to the calling God had given me. Even now, I knew that whatever the outcome on this mountain, life doesn't end on earth. This is just the beginning.

•

I prepared for the next leg of the descent, which involved more than a mile of down-climbing and 20-plus pitches of rappelling. My pack was heavier now, with the extra bottle of oxygen, but I put on my pack with renewed determination.

The last section down to the South Col was pretty steep, so I decided to use my figure-eight to rappel straight down. I had to be careful to hold my figure-eight securely as I pulled excess rope through the belaying device. It would be easy to drop it, and if I did, it was likely I'd never see it again. Another challenge was connecting the small loop into my locking carabiner on my harness—all without the luxury of being able to see what I was doing. Fortunately I'd had a couple of decades of experience using belaying devices, so I was attuned to the sound and feel of the carabiner when it snapped in. Beyond that, I simply had to trust my gear without being able to check it over visually. It was all about trust without seeing . . . kind of like faith.

As I made my way down the remaining 1,500 sheer vertical feet, something went very wrong. About 20 yards below the Balcony, I began to suffocate as my mask collapsed around my face. I couldn't breathe, and within seconds I became light headed. *Don't pass out!* I willed myself.

I ripped the mask from my face and gasped for air. Then I pulled my oxygen regulator close to my face. I was completely out of supplemental oxygen. And I still had a long way to go.

I anchored myself to an ice screw, dropped to my knees, and wept. I knelt there in the death zone, more desperate than I'd ever been, and surrendered my heart to God. "Please help me," I whispered. "I can't do this alone."

It was then that I experienced a true miracle.

At that moment, 2,000 feet below, Bill and Lakpa were near the Geneva Spur. They were getting increasingly worried about me, as six hours had passed with no word from Pasang or me. I found out later that Pasang was in his tent at the South Col without a radio, watching diligently for any signs of life from higher on the mountain. No one else had made a summit attempt that day on either side of Everest, so any movement above 26,000 feet would have to be me.

Bill and Lakpa ran through every possible scenario about what might have happened to me as they made their way toward the South Col. Bill wondered if he should try to contact JoAnna—and what he might say to her.

They climbed over the Geneva Spur and looked up at the summit of Mount Everest, scanning from one side to the other for any indications of life. They saw a form near the Balcony but couldn't tell if it was a climber or a rock. The only way to tell the difference at high altitudes is to watch the object for a while. If it doesn't move, it's pretty safe to classify it as a rock. They weren't sure, but they thought there had been small movements over time. They pressed on, climbing the last quarter mile into the death zone.

Thousands of miles around the earth, another miracle was happening. I didn't hear about it until weeks after my return, but after I pieced the stories together, it was undeniable that God was at work.

At her scrapbooking convention in Redmond, Washington, JoAnna felt high anxiety knowing that I was attempting my summit that day. She went back to her hotel room and pleaded with God on my behalf. "God, I lift Brian up to you, wherever he is," she cried. "I'm so worried about him, but I believe you can protect him."

At that precise moment I was kneeling down too—without oxygen and near the end of my rope. After my return, I heard countless stories from people who were jolted from sleep or whatever else they were doing and felt compelled to pray for me. Some people who didn't even know me told me they weren't sure why, but they'd felt a sudden urge to lift me up right at my moment of need.

It's true, I realized later. *I really wasn't alone on that mountain. Through the miracle of prayer, all these people were virtually assisting me in my descent.*

These are just a couple of the notes I received from people after my return:

> On Saturday morning, I went for a solo bike ride. I felt like God was really pressing me to pray for you. I'd been praying for you the whole trip, but that was the first time that I felt God telling me that I needed to stop and pray for you. My prayer was that you would receive the power and strength you needed from God to move when you needed to. I prayed that you would encounter a point on your summit push where you would need a boost to power through something.
>
> God is good, and I'm glad you take him with you when you go climbing. He is an okay partner to have around!
>
> David Heyting (family friend)
>
> I had followed your expedition from the beginning, and I was amazed that someone I knew would attempt something so difficult. I followed your blogs and got updates through JoAnna and on Facebook. In some very small way, I felt like I was there with you. On Thursday of the week you summited, I was asked to give a devotional on "radical faith" for our

women's Bible study. I was sure I was supposed to mention you.

One night while you were on your expedition, I awoke from a dead sleep at 1:30 a.m. (PST). I don't know how to explain it other than to say I just knew I was supposed to pray for you. I grabbed my phone and checked Facebook to see if there were any new updates. The last post from JoAnna said that you were going to attempt the summit, but there hadn't been anything new for many hours.

I prayed that God would give you the strength to continue wherever you were and that you would know you weren't alone. I was never afraid for you, but I didn't realize until later how close you would come to not making it home. To see you come back changed—physically, emotionally, and spiritually—has been simply amazing.

I didn't know the timing of my prayers and your experience until I heard you share at church the week you returned. Your journey is an inspiration to me—not just what you were able to do, but also the love and support your wife has for you (and her ultimate dependence on God). Your story is confirmation that there is nowhere we can go where God isn't with us. It's also a reminder to me that he really does answer our prayers!

Michelle Mumford (friend from church)

After uttering that desperate cry for help, I experienced something unlike anything I'd ever even seen before. I'm not sure I can entirely explain what happened, but all at once I felt a surge of energy and life come over me, and it felt like someone was helping me to my feet. While remaining anchored to the mountain, I removed my pack, my oxygen mask still half hanging from my face. I detached the hose from the depleted bottle, removed the canister Pasang had left for me, and attached the regulator. I don't even know why I attempted it again after it had been useless the last time I'd tried, but the moment I held it up, I felt air blowing against my face!

I reattached my mask and closed my eyes, sucking in several deep, slow breaths. I felt warmth course through my body and spread down to my fingers and toes. Life was reentering my limbs, burning through my body in a painful—but good—way. I stood up straight again, not even realizing I'd been hunched over until that moment. And then I noticed something else astonishing: when I looked up from the oxygen canister, I could tell that my vision had improved slightly. Everything around me was still a massive whiteout, but I was able to focus a little better on close-range objects. I'd heard about climbers who didn't have snow blindness but whose vision had been affected by altitude alone, so it was possible the oxygen was helping my eyes.

Without giving myself time to overthink it, I secured my figure-eight to the fixed line and rappelled down multiple pitches. It was so surreal that part of me wondered if I was hallucinating. I tried to study my watch to see what time it was, but the numbers were a blur. It was hard to know how much time had passed, but I knew I needed to maximize my renewed life and get down to safety. I had no way of knowing if this burst of energy would be temporary, like an adrenaline rush, or if it would stick with me, so I wanted to take advantage of it.

I continued to rappel down the massive face of Everest. I became more efficient about coming in and out of the anchors by feel, but I made sure to check them carefully each time before releasing my safety. My body was starting to feel heavy on my legs, and some of the slopes were turning slushy. I couldn't afford to get sloppy under these conditions.

At one point I stopped to try to get my bearings. I thought I was about 500 feet from the edge of the South Col. I squinted out into the vast, white terrain, looking for landmarks and wondering if anyone could see me.

Nothing seemed familiar, and I felt panic creeping in again. *Where am I?* I wondered. *Did I rappel down the wrong mountain face?*

I took some deep breaths, trying to stay calm.

I looked up and contemplated climbing up again to see if I'd gone the wrong way. That should have been my first indication that all the exposure to the thin air was starting to affect my mind.

I checked the altimeter on my watch, but it was too blurry for me to read. Down in the distance, I thought I saw pockets of orange, which I assumed were tents. And it seemed like the silhouette of Lhotse Face was in front of me. But without being able to see the outline of Everest behind me, I couldn't be sure. I decided it was futile to try to question where I was any longer, so I rappelled down toward the bottom. I'd head toward what I assumed was high camp. If I made it, I'd just ask to sleep in someone's tent and sort things out later.

I was relieved to reach the ice bulge, the area entering

the South Col. *I must be going the right way!* I thought. I came off the rappelling gear and switched back to my safety line. I was now on the last quarter mile from the edge of Everest to where our tents were located, on the far side of the South Col. As I walked across the ice field, I staggered, trying to put one foot in front of the other. I was so close to safety, but it still felt like I had so far to go. *Will I actually survive this?*

As I walked the quarter mile through camp, I started hallucinating, thinking the blurry rocks in the distance were people waving at me. As I neared them, I would stop and squint my eyes, trying to focus on the people. *What are they doing so far out on the South Col?* I wondered. As I got closer, I realized they weren't people at all. Then I'd look down at them and say, "Stupid rock!" I was so exhausted I was getting delirious.

Did I die up here? I asked myself. *Surely this can't be heaven. If this is heaven, then heaven stinks!*

Then, out of nowhere, someone appeared and grabbed me in a huge hug.

"Brian, you're alive!" It was Pasang's voice. "I'm sorry for leaving you there."

I assured him that he hadn't abandoned me—that it had been a mutual decision, and it had made sense to both of us at the time. Nobody could have predicted what would happen over the course of the day.

"Don't sweat it, dude," I said.

I couldn't stop the tears from streaming down my face. *I made it!* I told myself over and over. *I'm alive! I really made it!*

Pasang later sent me a Facebook message with his memory of that day:

That morning I saw Brian up high, slowly coming
down from the South Summit. When I saw him,
I thought he had a problem because he was walking
with great difficulty. I wondered if he was having
trouble with his eyes, so I went to meet him with my
extra sunglasses, plus hot juice and biscuits. When
I met him near the South Col, I see his eyes cannot
work. Snow blind.

•

"You don't look good," Pasang told me. "I'm glad you made
it. Let's get you to the tent."

I gave Pasang an abbreviated version of what had happened and updated him about the current condition of my
eyes. Then we headed back across the ice field toward camp.

Pasang moved quickly across the South Col, and I struggled to keep up. All of a sudden he was gone—presumably
into one of the tents—but they all blended together in my
foggy vision. After tripping over a bunch of rocks in search
of my tent, I decided I needed help.

"Pasang," I called. "Where are you?"

"Over here," he called. His voice was coming from behind
me. I spun around and fell backward into the open doorway of our tent. He helped me remove my climbing gear—
my crampons, my harness, and my pack. It felt good to be
relieved of the load I'd been carrying for so long.

"What time did you reach summit?" he asked.

"Around six o'clock in the morning."

"I knew it," Pasang replied. "That's what I said we
would do."

After watching the mountain from his tent since early

sunrise, Pasang had decided I must be in trouble up there. He was planning to go up and find me as soon as he gained his energy back and felt well enough to make the climb.

I handed him my camera so he could flip through the digital pictures I'd taken at 29,035 feet. It had been just hours earlier, but it felt like a lifetime ago.

It was warm in the tent, so I dropped my suit halfway, put on my sunglasses, and leaned back on my sleeping bag. That's when it really started to hit me. *I almost died up there,* I thought. *Thank you, God, for keeping me alive.*

I don't think Pasang noticed that I was weeping behind my sunglasses—or maybe he did, but he wanted to give me some privacy. I don't think my body had ever been so fatigued in my entire life.

Somewhere in the background, I heard the welcome sound of Pasang boiling water to make some tea and soup.

I thought about JoAnna back home and hoped she wasn't worried. Our communications were relayed from our radios on the mountain down to base camp and then back to Kathmandu, where Sagar, our Nepalese contact, would contact Bill's wife. The only thing people back home knew at this point was that I'd summited and that I was safe at high camp. Sagar didn't know about my blind descent, which meant JoAnna didn't know about it either. But she might wonder why it was taking so long for her to hear anything.

I later read her journal entry reflecting back on what she was going through while I was descending solo.

Before Brian left, he arranged for me to go to a
scrapbooking retreat. We had no idea at the time that
it would end up being the same dates as his summit

attempt. I got there on Friday, May 13, and Brian had called a few days earlier to let me know he'd be making the attempt on May 14. Bill's wife called that morning at nine o'clock, letting me know they'd try to summit that night.

I had told a couple of friends at the retreat about Brian's expedition, and word spread quickly. That afternoon people started asking how the trip was going, but I hadn't heard anything. Others around me were starting to grow anxious and impatient, but I felt peace about the whole thing, so I stayed pretty calm.

On all the other climbs Brian had done in the past, he'd rented a satellite phone so we could stay in touch. He always called from the summit so I could share the moment with him. No matter the circumstances, he always managed to find a way to contact me. This time, though, I knew Brian's phone didn't work past base camp, so I didn't expect to hear from him unless he managed to borrow someone else's phone to call from the summit.

I explained the situation to the women and said it was unlikely I'd hear anything even if he'd summited. It wasn't until dinnertime that I started to get worried. All at once, this overwhelming sense of doom came over me. I was checking my phone constantly, and I couldn't focus on scrapbooking any longer.

After dinner, I decided to go to my room to think and pray, but I mostly ended up crying. I just had this gut feeling that something was very wrong. I talked to Bill's wife again, but she didn't know anything.

I didn't sleep much that night—I kept waking up to check my phone and pray. But incredibly, the next morning I felt an overwhelming peace even though I still hadn't heard anything. Somehow I knew that things would be okay.

On Sunday I left the retreat and headed home. I picked Emily up, and we went to a Girl Scouts horseback riding event. I still hadn't heard anything at this point, so I e-mailed and texted everyone I could think of to pray for Brian.

At 9:30 p.m. Bill's wife called to tell me that Brian had successfully summited and was at Camp IV. That was all we knew at that point.

As I lay in my tent taking in oxygen, my eyes started to swell shut. After hours of having to fight the urge to close my eyes, I was finally able to give in and get some much-needed rest.

Before I had a chance to drift off to sleep, Bill unzipped the vestibule and dove through the open doorway to give me a hug.

"Congratulations!" he said. "Lakpa and I were so worried about you. Brian, only you could survive something like that." He shook his head in amazement and disbelief. "Only you."

I later got Bill's perspective on my summit day when I read his blog entry.

May 22, 2011

Around noon, I really was starting to worry. Most strong climbers can descend from the summit in three or four hours, and Brian was clearly in that category. It was now going on seven hours from his summit call, and there was still no word from him or Pasang.

All kinds of scenarios started to play out in my head. What would I tell JoAnna, Brian's wife?

Every time someone descended from the Geneva Spur in a down suit, I held my breath, hoping it was Brian or Pasang.

As Lakpa and I approached the Geneva Spur, we saw a small black dot near the Balcony. *Is that Brian? Or maybe Pasang?* I wondered. *Perhaps it's just a rock. I couldn't tell.* It may have been moving, but if so, it was going very slowly.

Then, as we traversed farther, I looked again. It had to be Brian—he was alive![1]

"So what was it like?" Bill went on. He wanted to hear all the details of my summit and impossible descent.

I didn't have the energy to give him the full story at that point, but I managed to say simply, "I soloed Mount Everest and then descended blind." I swallowed, trying to hide my tears. "I witnessed a miracle up there."

CHAPTER 9

ESCAPING THE DEATH ZONE

Those who hope in the LORD will renew their strength.
They will soar on wings like eagles; they will run and not grow weary,
they will walk and not be faint.

ISAIAH 40:31

LONG AFTER the sun set, I jerked awake, wracked with claustrophobia. With the oxygen mask strapped to my face and my eyes swollen shut, it felt like the walls of the tent were closing in around me. I tried to pry my eyes open, but the secreted fluids had crusted over, effectively gluing my eyes shut. It felt like grains of sand were stuck under my eyelids, scratching my eyelids with each tiny movement I made.

Bill sat on the other side of the tent and prepared for his summit attempt. He told me later that I kept waking up, grabbing my camera, forcing my eyes open with my fingers, and making the flash go off to find out if I could see anything. He kept asking if I was okay, but I would just silently take a close-range picture of myself and go back to sleep. I don't have any recollection of any of this, but it was confirmed a few days later when I downloaded the contents of my camera. The pictures were disturbing—a series of close-ups of my glassed-over, unfocused eyes.

Bill attempted the summit that night but had to turn back just shy of the Balcony due to equipment issues and high winds. He arrived at the tent around two o'clock in the morning, unzipped the vestibule, and shone his headlamp inside. I woke up immediately, the bright light like fire to my sensitive eyes, even through my closed lids. I squeezed my eyes more tightly shut, which caused scratching and more pain. Finally, I covered my eyes with a buff to try to block out the light.

As Bill removed his climbing gear, I overheard his conversation with Pasang.

"I'm not worried about turning back on my summit attempt," Bill said. "All that matters now is getting Brian back down."

I was glad he'd made it down safely, but I hoped he wouldn't be perpetually disappointed about his failed attempt.

I slept off and on for about 15 hours, and by morning, my face was a train wreck, with both eyes swollen and painfully scratchy. We got moving as soon as the sun lit up the tent so we could descend Lhotse Face all the way down to Camp II. Pasang and Bill helped me get my harness on and packed my sleeping bag for me. I felt around the tent and tried to pack up the rest of my stuff, but I ended up leaving my favorite sunglasses in one of the side pockets. Fortunately Pasang let me use his extra goggles for the descent, and I'd be able to retrieve my backup pair of sunglasses at base camp.

I found my way out of the tent and stood by myself for a moment. It was cold, with frequent gusts of wind, but the sun was quickly warming up the mountain. I was in physical pain, but I was also at peace somehow. As I stood there trying to regain equilibrium without my vision, I had an underlying certainty that things were going to be okay.

I heard Lakpa come over. "Congratulations on summit!" he said as he strapped on my crampons. "How are your eyes?"

"Very painful," I said. "But I'll be okay."

I fumbled my way to the edge of camp to urinate before our big descent. I tripped over some rocks but eventually managed to find a place away from the tents. It was amazing how difficult even this basic task was without the benefit of being able to see. I probably did more damage to myself than to the mountain, but there are just some things you don't want to accept help for.

Before we began our descent, Bill said, "Would you take a picture of me with Everest in the background?"

Are you serious? I thought. *You want a blind guy taking a photo for you?* But I aimed and shot, and Bill said the end result wasn't too shabby, all things considered.

Pasang, Bill, and I headed down, with Lakpa to follow a little later. I'd become pretty proficient at climbing blind the day before, but I was grateful to have Pasang ahead of me. Through the blinding brightness, I was able to make out his blue down suit and follow it. It also helped to have Bill's and Pasang's voice commands to follow. Even so, I held tight to the fixed lines.

The initial traverse down to the Geneva Spur was gradual, but I took my time, ensuring that each foot was in front of the other and that I was always attached to the fixed rope. It was rocky, so I made my way cautiously, careful not to twist an ankle. I switched to my figure-eight to rappel down the other side of the spur, which was covered in windswept snow. I knew it would be difficult to gain purchase with crampons in that type of snow, and I hoped the figure-eight would help steady me.

My eyes were in severe pain, and I struggled to keep them open. I needed some sort of lubricant, but I had nothing other than my constant tears. Blinking was so painful that I tried to prevent my eyelids from closing at all, since each time they did, they scraped hard against my eyes. After a while I wouldn't be able to hold back any longer, and I'd blink and cry out in pain.

As we moved toward the Yellow Band, I put my head down and tried to pour all my energy into each step of the long downward stretch. Later I realized that this was the same place where the snow-blind climber was being helped down two days earlier, but at the time, I was so focused I didn't let myself think about the connection. It took all the discipline I had to concentrate on keeping my balance on the unstable surface.

It was difficult to rappel over the Yellow Band since the anchor points were scattered in various locations on angled rocks. And since it was a rock rappel, we had to go one at a time—Bill and Pasang couldn't stay there to help me and make sure I was okay. They rappelled down the other side and waited for me there. I was pretty much all over the place, trying to keep my balance and not slip off the rocks. With clear vision, I wouldn't have had much trouble, but if I over-shot one of the anchors, it would have been impossible to feed the rope back into my figure-eight with my full body weight pulling on it. I rappelled down and stopped a foot above the anchor, finding the appropriate location by sliding my free hand on top of the rope. Then I attached my figure-eight on the line below while remaining attached to the line above with my safety carabiner. I slipped a few times on the uneven surface, but thankfully I avoided getting hurt.

We descended over a couple of icy areas on 80-degree slopes. I was careful to kick in full crampon purchase, as a slip there could result in broken bones or an uncontrolled fall. After a few hours of careful downhill steps, we arrived at Camp III, where Dawa was gathering supplies to take down to Camp II.

"Congratulations, Brian!" he exclaimed, giving me a hug.

"Thanks, Dawa," I said, turning my head in the direction of his voice.

At Camp III, we got some water, ate a snack, and reapplied sunscreen. We encountered several climbers who were heading up Lhotse Face. One by one they stopped to congratulate me on my summit. They'd been shocked to find out from Bill what had happened on my descent. I didn't say much about it, not wanting to scare them about their own summit attempt, but the word had spread quickly.

We continued the last few miles of our descent to Camp II. A couple of sections were steep slopes covered with solid blue glacial ice that would have been tough to navigate even with full vision. My steel points barely pierced the icy surface, which didn't give me much confidence, but I made it down without incident.

At one point when I was struggling with my figure-eight, a European climber who was heading up saw that I was having trouble. She reached down, removed my carabiner from my belaying device, pulled the rope through, and clipped it back on.

A couple of groups were crossing the bergschrund at the base of Lhotse, and it was tricky to navigate around them with my compromised vision. In certain spots where I knew it would take me longer, I stood still and had everyone else go by me. They told me to go ahead, but I insisted on waiting. I knew how long the drop was and how narrow the passage ahead would be, so I wanted to go slowly and not take any chances.

The last obstacle before the Western Cwm was a bent aluminum ladder someone had placed across a widening crevasse. It had a single fixed rope on the left side, so I carefully placed each crampon on the rungs of the ladder and pulled my way across. On the way up, I had high centered my boots between the crampon spikes to cross. Without the advantage of vision, I had to rely almost entirely on touch, so it helped to have full contact with the ladder. Even so, the single rope set me off balance. I bent my knees to steady myself, like I might do while surfing or snowboarding. I took each step very slowly, shifting my weight appropriately whenever I transferred from one foot to the other. I made it across without incident and then forward rappelled, with my safety connected to the fixed rope, until the rope ran out and I was on flatter terrain. I breathed a sigh of exhausted relief. *I made it down Lhotse Face!* The flat ground of the Western Cwm felt foreign—almost like walking on dry land after being on a boat for an extended time.

Days before I had cached my trekking poles at the bottom of Lhotse Face. I found the spot where I'd left them, but only one of the poles remained. I'd have to make do with one. It was disappointing, but I took courage from the fact that the only thing separating me from the safety of my Camp II tent was a downhill mile. My stomach was growling and I felt fatigue settling over my body, and I was grateful that Dawa had gone down before us to start lunch.

I was off rope now, with no fixed lines, but that didn't mean I was clear of all dangers. There were plenty of hidden crevasses that would be especially difficult to notice in my present condition. Bill and Pasang had gotten ahead of me, and I started moving even slower. I'd take one step and then bend down to try to focus on the next spot to move my foot. It was midday, and with the sun glaring on the white snow, the landscape was so bright it might as well have been fluorescent. The way the Western Cwm is positioned, with its valley full of snow, there's nothing to contrast against the white—it's just pure white on pure white. I tried using my one trekking pole to steady myself. As Bill stepped over a two-foot-wide crevasse, he saw me struggling and waited for me there.

"Grab my hand," he said, guiding me over the crevasse. I held his hand the rest of the way across to Camp II, not only to help me walk more efficiently but also to avoid any obstacles in the path. We laughed, talking about how we couldn't think of any other circumstances in which we'd willingly hold hands with another guy. The unexpected light moment provided some much-needed laughter, releasing the built-up tension I'd been holding in for some time.

Veronique, the French-Canadian climber from our group, met us a few hundred yards from camp.

When she saw me, she gave me a big hug. "Congratulations, Brian!"

"Thanks," I said. "I made it down blind." I hoped no one could see the tears forming behind my goggles.

She paused, processing what she'd just heard. "You're a machine!" She grabbed my pack and carried it the rest of the way to camp for me.

As I entered Camp II, I could see the blur of several blue and orange tents. I couldn't be sure, but it seemed like my right eye was regaining some focus. I navigated across the rocky terrain, finally reaching our cooking tent, where Dawa was preparing lunch. I walked in, using my pole in exaggerated fashion, tapping it from side to side on the snow.

"Brian, at least you still have your sense of humor," one of the Sherpas said, laughing.

The aroma of the warm meal Dawa was preparing made my empty stomach ache. I sat down on one of the rock slabs and came off oxygen for the last time. Now that I was able to let down my guard, the events of the past few days suddenly washed over me, and I wept into my hands.

I'd been to the edge of death and back, and now I was finally in the safety of our Camp II tent. After wiping my tears, I removed my harness and crampons, untied my boots, and ate a hearty lunch of Spam, sardines, potatoes, and bread.

Back in 2009, I'd had another experience of staring death in the face. During my expedition to Denali, I'd been pinned down at high camp for a week due to extreme weather. After spending several days carrying 60 pounds in my backpack and towing another 70 pounds in a sled, our group made it to 14,000 feet. We then made multiple carries up the fixed lines and across the steep ridge to high camp, at 17,200 feet. That's when we were hit with 70-plus-mile-per-hour winds and were forced to stay in the relative safety of our tents.

It was the coldest place I'd ever been, and it was the first time I'd really had to survive in such harsh weather conditions. It was so cold that I could see my breath freeze into ice crystals at the small opening in my sleeping bag. The temperatures dropped so low during the night that I even heard the metal pots freezing and cracking. Back then I didn't have the quality of gear I had for Everest, so my body constantly felt like an ice cube, and I was concerned about getting frostbite.

As physically taxing as the experience was, it was even more intense mentally, because I had to lie still for a week with little movement other than rolling over in my sleeping bag and praying that the weather would calm down. While the rest of our group stayed hunkered down in tents, one climber tried to solo the mountain. We all tried to advise him against it, but he refused to change his mind. His body was never found. Eventually the rest of us made a summit attempt, but we had to turn back 1,000 feet shy of the summit due to high winds. It was disappointing not to complete our goal after working so hard to achieve it, but it was also a good day to live.

●

After lunch, there was one thing I was desperate to do: call JoAnna. I wasn't sure what she'd heard—if she knew I'd summited or if she'd found out anything about my snow blindness—and I was anxious to fill her in. Veronique let me use her satellite phone, and I stumbled across the snow, halfway between the cooking tent and my personal tent, so I could have a little privacy. I had no idea what I would say to JoAnna. So much had taken place since I'd talked to her last, and I was still a wreck—physically and emotionally. It was late back in Seattle, but she answered almost immediately.

The moment I heard the sound of her voice, I broke into tears.

"Hi, honey!" I could hear the relief in her voice. "Can you hear me? Are you there?"

I tried to respond, but I was so choked up I couldn't get a word out. I swallowed a lump so big my throat ached. "I soloed the summit," I said. "And I'm blind. I'll call you tomorrow."

The phone went silent for a few seconds.

"Is the phone cutting out?" she asked.

"No, I just can't stop crying," I said. "I'll call tomorrow. I love you!"

I hung up, and then the tears really started. JoAnna had sounded strong on the phone, but she and I both knew that I still had to get through the Khumbu Icefall.

As I replayed our conversation in my mind, it hit me: she didn't know I was temporarily blind. She probably thought I was permanently blind. I wished I could have a do over of the phone call so I could say something to calm her and put her mind at ease.

After returning the phone to Veronique, I made my way to my tent. The tent was hot now, with the midday sun shining on it, so I fell into the vestibule and removed my sweaty down suit for the last time. I felt my way through the tent toward my air mattress and sleeping bag. After blowing up the mattress and uncompressing my bag from the stuff sack, I lay down to relax. If it hadn't been for the extreme pain in my eyes, it would have felt like heaven to be able to rest like this.

All at once I sat up, remembering the photos of my family that I'd stashed in the side pockets of the tent. I found one of Emily and Jordan and held it inches from my face. I tried hard to focus, but I couldn't see anything beyond a couple of blurry images. Even so, I knew from memory the exact details of the picture. With tears streaming down my face, I held the picture to my chest, which was the closest I could get at the moment to hugging my precious kids. Even though they were halfway around the world, my family felt so close to me in that moment.

I thanked God for delivering me from death so I'd be able to hug JoAnna and the kids in the flesh again. "Thank you, Lord," I prayed. "Thank you for sparing my life. Thank you for giving me another chance. Thank you for this gift of life. Please help me to get down the mountain safely so I can return to my family. Thank you, thank you."

I lay down and dozed off for about an hour. When I awoke, I fumbled around to repack my gear so I'd be ready to leave early the next morning. We were planning to leave in the dark to reduce the pain the bright sun inflicted on my damaged eyes. I packed my gear into a stuff sack and gathered all my loose items into my pack.

Bill and I sat in the dining tent waiting to eat our last dinner above base camp. We planned to go to sleep early and wake up before sunrise. He offered me some ointment, but since it wasn't specifically intended for eyes, I decided not to risk it. Other than that, we didn't talk much. I was reliving my summit and my dramatic descent, which still seemed somewhat surreal to me. Bill didn't say anything, but as his mood grew more and more regretful, I wondered if he was reliving his failed summit attempt with a bunch of what-ifs.

"Bill, this may not be any of my business," I said, "but if you feel like you're going to regret not making another attempt on Mount Everest, you should consider staying."

He looked at me without responding, so I continued.

"You could always rest a week at base camp and then head up for another attempt."

Not everyone has to make it to the top, but I didn't want him to wish one day that he'd stayed longer and made a second attempt. He'd come so far already.

He thanked me, but he just wasn't in the right place mentally to consider another attempt.

Our plan was to get down to base camp, call our wives, and then head down to Pheriche. We'd figure out our next steps there depending on how my eyesight was doing. My right eye was already starting to clear up a bit, but my left eye was badly damaged, and I was struggling to see straight.

I'd learned in first-aid training for AIRR that eyes work in coordination, as the muscles try to keep both eyes aligned. That's why we were taught to cover both eyes in an eye injury. For example, if a knife were stuck in a victim's eyes, we'd cover both of them, since if one eye moves, the other moves with it. Now I was on the other side of my training—as the one with the injury, not the one treating it.

We ate an early dinner of dal bhat and then retreated to our individual tents, where we staged our gear for an early morning departure.

I lay in bed until well after dark, too excited to sleep. The reality of what I had accomplished was finally starting to sink in. When you plan and dream about such an event, you never really understand the true magnitude of the challenge. And when it finally becomes a reality, it feels utterly unbelievable. As both the traumatic events and the climactic moments replayed in my mind, I sobbed throughout the night, filled with a mixture of gratitude, joy, and delayed fear. I had compartmentalized my emotions to get down the mountain alive, and now the compartment had burst wide open. The tears were welcome, painful as they were—and so was sleep, when it finally came.

•

Around 4 a.m. Bill and I were both awake and ready to move. I got dressed for the descent and finished packing my gear. I slowly crunched across the frozen snow and staged my pack near the cooking tent. The darkness gave my eyes some relief, but I felt searing pain anytime an occasional headlamp pointed in my direction.

Bill and I sat on a cold slab in the tent while Dawa warmed water for drinks. After a quick breakfast, I thanked Dawa and gave him a tip, knowing it might be the last time I saw him.

"Thank you for everything," I said, giving him a hug. "I'll miss you."

"Congratulations on summit, Brian!" he said, thumping me on the back. "Go back home to see your family."

I picked up my pack, strapped it around my waist, and headed down the hill.

I started moving more efficiently as the vision in my right eye gradually returned. I tried keeping my right eye open and my left one closed to help with equilibrium, but I still felt off balance. I needed to stay alert, because the Western Cwm is littered with hidden, snow-covered crevasses. It was more important than ever for me to stay close to my team and listen for their warnings.

The first half of the trek was pretty straightforward, but I knew that as I got closer to Camp I, I would have to cross ladders and crevasses and eventually descend the 30-plus ladders through the Khumbu Icefall. Much too soon, the sun started to peek out over the mountaintops ahead. I was wearing Pasang's extra pair of tinted goggles, but I knew it wouldn't be enough to protect against the midday sun. I picked up the pace, trying to move as quickly as possible under the circumstances.

Then we came to a step-over crevasse measuring a couple of feet across, 20 yards wide, and hundreds of feet deep. I grabbed the fixed rope and connected my safety as a precaution before easily stepping across.

I could feel gravity on our side as we made our way downhill, and perhaps the even greater advantage was the decreasing altitude. With each step lower, the air thickened, filling my lungs with life and energy. *Every step is bringing me closer to home and my family,* I kept telling myself.

The first ladder I approached on the Western Cwm was a single, with one fixed line to help with balance. Since my equilibrium was still off, I relied purely on feel to get across. Each step was like a puzzle to solve, with the points of my crampons gripping the aluminum rungs. I probably would have been better off without the rope, but I held on tightly and bent my knees to lower my center of gravity. With each step, the rope pulled me off center, and my heart kept jumping into my throat.

My legs were shaky, and I certainly wasn't fast or graceful, but I managed to make my way across. I opted out of the five-ladder crossing and took the 15-minute walk around instead. That route wasn't easy either, as it circumnavigated the deep crevasse and then switched back and forth through sections that measured just a few feet wide and over 100 feet deep. Any slip there would certainly ruin my day.

•

Entering Camp I felt like a big accomplishment, but it also was a reminder of what was ahead of me: the icefall. We took a quick break for water and a snack and then made our way up and out of the Western Cwm. At the top of the icefall, we had to switch back and forth to avoid major obstacles, so I was clipping in and out of the fixed lines the entire route.

When I reached a crossing that had been made of four ladders the last time I was there, I was relieved to discover that avalanches had wiped it out a week ago and there was now a new route. Instead of having to venture across a bridge of four ladders, we climbed down a series of ladders that were bolted to the ice. Once at the bottom, we crossed a flat section—right through the heart of the crevasse—before climbing up another set of ladders to get out.

I clung to the rope as I found each rung with my crampon points. My spikes kept getting pinned between the rungs and the ice wall, so I had to be cautious when freeing them so I wouldn't lose my balance and fall backward. When I got to the two tied-together ladders that were leading out of the crevasse, I noticed that they weren't exactly straight. They slanted to the right, and when I moved to the second ladder, the whole thing swung sideways, barely attached to the ice wall with a single ice screw. I held my lifeline securely and pulled my way to the top, where I stopped to hydrate my parched mouth.

I looked ahead of me, testing my vision. Close objects were becoming more visible through my right eye, but everything beyond 20 feet was still a complete blur. I wanted to be able to move faster, but I knew that frustration isn't a productive emotion, so I picked myself up, grabbed the fixed rope, and continued toward my destination.

We had to cross a handful of ladders and crevasses, and I was grateful that Pasang stayed near me during this portion of the journey. He crossed the ladders ahead of me and tightened the safety lines from the other side.

When we came to a maze of fallen seracs, I could tell immediately that there was no way around it: I'd have to rappel down. *Every obstacle you make it through is one more obstacle closer to your destination,* I told myself.

As I came around the final corner to enter the gauntlet of ice, I surveyed the scene, trying to figure out what had happened. From what I could gather, an avalanche of ice must have wiped out that section in the last few days. It looked like a bomb had been dropped in the center of the Khumbu Icefall. Ultimately, though, the avalanche worked to our advantage, because it meant we had a few hundred yards of flat, open walking. This leg of our journey ended up taking us only 15 minutes rather than the usual 45. *God, is this another one of your miracles?* I couldn't help but wonder.

In no time, we were through the valley of snow and ice. We'd reached the midpoint of the icefall.

The rest of the way down was uneventful, which is exactly what I'd been hoping for. I got into a rhythm of clipping in and out of the fixed lines and cautiously making my way up and over the fallen seracs. The sun was beaming down in full force, but its negative effects were balanced out by the oxygen-rich air, which was recharging me by the minute. When I reached the end of the ice and the beginning of the rocky base camp path, I felt relief course through my body.

As I bent down to remove my crampons, I said to myself over and over, *I made it! I really made it!*

Images of what I'd seen and what I'd survived flashed through my mind, but I forced myself to compartmentalize them. I was on a mission to get home, and I didn't want anything to distract me. I figured I'd have plenty of time for that in the days to come.

•

Bill and I radioed down to base camp, letting the Sherpa crew know we'd arrived. Everyone was very excited about my summit and our safe return. One by one, the crew came up to me, shaking my hand and embracing me. My success was their success, which made the moment special for all of us.

We ate a quick bite and rehydrated before escaping to our tents. My first priority now that my phone had reception was to call JoAnna. I talked to her for 30 minutes, describing every detail of my ordeal. I wished she could have been there in person since I knew there were parts of the story that were hard for her to hear, but I was so glad to finally be able to share this with her.

"I was so worried you were permanently blind," she told me. "I'm so glad you're okay." I heard her ragged breath, and once again I regretted my brief words on Veronique's phone.

"Now you just have to make it out," she said.

Emily and Jordan were already in bed, so I asked her to tell them that I'd climbed Everest and was on my way home. I knew I couldn't tell the kids all the details for years to come since it would only cause them unnecessary concern—both now and when I went on future climbs. More than ever, I wanted to be home to hold JoAnna and the kids tight, to let them know how much I loved them and how thankful I was for them. I would have to wait for five more days.

After I reluctantly hung up, I packed up my base camp gear so the Sherpa porter could start heading down. Our plan was to get down to Pheriche that day, to Namche Bazaar (or farther) the second day, and then fly out of Lukla the following day. It was Bill's 40th birthday, so the Sherpa team made a birthday cake for him and a summit cake for me. We were in a rush to go, but we didn't want to be in such a hurry that we brushed past this celebratory moment and the company of our Sherpa crew.

I fumbled around with my camera, trying to focus with one eye open, but between my poor vision and the damage my camera had sustained from the cold temperatures on the summit, the photos didn't do the moment much justice. The pictures of my cake were little more than a bright yellow blur, but at least I was able to mark the occasion.

Then it was time to say good-bye to our Sherpa family.

"Thank you for all your help and for the great conversations," I told them, giving each one an individual tip, plus most of my gear—down jackets, pants, and booties. "I will miss talking to you. Please enjoy returning to your families."

•

As I left base camp for the final time, I turned back, trying to freeze the image in my mind. *Remember this!* I told myself, willing my mind to memorize every part of the scene.

As I made my way toward Lukla, which would take me to Kathmandu and then to Bangkok, on to Taiwan, and finally home to Seattle, I thought about the final blog post

I'd write as soon as I had a chance to sit down somewhere with Internet access. I'd have to write it with one eye closed, but I knew exactly what I wanted to say.

May 17, 2011

First off, I'd like to apologize to JoAnna and my family for putting them through this worrisome two-month adventure. You've been very supportive, which I appreciate, but it was a risky endeavor, and I apologize for any pain and worry I may have caused you. What started as a major life goal ended as a fight for survival. I lived to tell about my nearly impossible scenario on Mount Everest only because of sheer determination to live and a miracle from God. . . . With God, anything is possible.[1]

LIFE AFTER EVEREST

Everyone who is a child of God conquers the world.
And this is the victory that conquers the world—our faith.

1 JOHN 5:4, NCV

AFTER MY 38-mile blind stagger through the Khumbu Valley, the rest of my journey home was a breeze. Many summiteers stay an extra night in Kathmandu and sign the wall in the Rum Doodle restaurant, but I was on a mission to get home as soon as possible.

It seemed surreal, after fighting for every inch of ground, to be covering more than 500 miles per hour while sitting in the back row of a Thai Airways flight. I'd lost 20 pounds, and I looked like I'd just taken second place in an intense mixed—martial arts battle. My eyes were swollen and black, and I had scars all across my face from extended periods of wearing an oxygen mask. Thankfully, my eyes weren't causing much pain anymore, although they were still sensitive to light. In terms of vision, my right eye still wasn't perfect, and everything through my left eye was a complete blur. I could see well enough, however, to notice that other passengers would look at me and then quickly avert their eyes.

It's really over. The thought brought a strange mixture of relief and disappointment—relief that I'd survived, and disappointment that the adventure was coming to an end. I couldn't wait to see my family again, but there was also some degree of letdown. The moment I'd been planning for, hoping for, and dreaming about for months was firmly behind me. It seemed impossible that I was sitting in a climate-controlled cabin, eating a meal that didn't involve Spam in any form, and resting without wondering if the walls around me would come down in the wind.

I looked around at the other passengers through my hazy eyes and wondered about their stories. *Nobody here knows what happened to me in the past few months,* I thought. *No one knows I experienced a miracle of Christ a mile into the death zone.* As I reclined in my seat, tears filled my eyes. *Heavenly Father,* I prayed silently, *thank you so much for delivering me from death. Thank you for getting me safely on this plane. Please give my family peace as I make my way home. And please restore my vision. Thank you, Lord. Amen.*

As I drifted off to sleep, I pictured the scene that would be awaiting me when I returned to Sea-Tac Airport. A group of friends would be there to welcome me, but most of all, I kept imagining running through the airport to embrace my family. My eyes were getting heavy as the cadence echoed through my mind one more time: *Emily, Jordan, JoAnna. Emily, Jordan, JoAnna.*

•

Once my plane finally landed in Seattle, several hours later than planned due to mechanical difficulties in Taiwan, I was bone tired but also filled with the adrenaline of a much-anticipated homecoming. It seemed to take forever to deplane, but I made my way as quickly as I could through the blurry Sea-Tac Airport.

The escalator to the arrival area was packed, so I raced up the stairs. There, waiting at the top, was my wife, looking more gorgeous than ever. We embraced bashfully, with tears streaming down our faces. Somehow two months apart had made us both more in love and more nervous around each other.

I was jet lagged and hungry, so we stopped at a McDonald's drive-through on the way home. Under normal circumstances, I'm not a fan of fast food, but after two months of freeze-dried dinners, my burger and fries tasted like a five-star dinner.

When we got home, the kids were sleeping, so I sneaked into Emily's and Jordan's rooms to kiss them on their foreheads. They were the most precious sights I'd ever laid eyes on—even more breathtaking than the Himalayan peaks I'd tried to capture with my camera lens.

The next morning, before I was fully conscious, the kids came running into our room to dive-bomb me in bed. Jordan kept staring at me through his long eyelashes, saying, "Daddy, Daddy, Daddy!" over and over again. Emily couldn't stop smiling as she recounted in detail everything she'd done for the past two months.

After I'd been home for a couple of days, JoAnna let me read her version of my return, which she'd written about in her journal.

May 21, 2011

Brian arrived home very late last night after his plane broke down in Taiwan. A friend came over to stay with the kids while I picked him up from the airport. I couldn't wait to see him—I've never anticipated an event so much in my life. The moment I saw him, everyone around me disappeared, and we held each other for a long time, both of us crying. My husband was finally home!

It was a surreal moment, knowing that he'd been through so much but that I'd been disconnected from most of it. He had come so close to death, and I knew I'd never be able to fully understand everything he'd experienced on that mountain. Nobody would. In that moment, I wasn't sure I ever wanted him to climb again. I was afraid he'd leave us forever.

•

It took a few days at home before my right eye returned to normal. I had to make a few visits to the ophthalmologist for my left eye, but after about a month, my cornea healed properly, and my vision returned.

My mind has taken longer to recover. I still deal with post-traumatic stress disorder when I give detailed accounts of my story. If I'm discussing Everest at a surface level, I'm able to keep my emotions in check by skipping over or downplaying the more horrific details. But when I give live presentations, I still break down when I talk about certain aspects of the descent.

When I describe my last radio call down to Bill and

Lakpa, I'm immediately drawn back to that moment of realization, knowing how close I came to never seeing my family again. And when I tell people about the time I ran out of oxygen at 27,500 feet and how I surrendered completely to God, that's when I really lose it. In that moment, I was given the gift of life and an unexplained miracle. I don't understand why I made it when so many others throughout the years have not. It's too mind boggling to comprehend, and the only thing I can do in response is to live as fully and gratefully as I can.

For someone who's used to living a quiet life, it feels strange to be thrust into the spotlight, especially since I'm just as flawed as the next guy. But for some reason God spared my life up there, and I've been given the task of sharing my story and helping others however I can. I may not feel worthy, but I don't want to waste the gift.

Ever since my return, I've been asked regularly if I'll keep climbing, and specifically if I'll continue to pursue the seven summits. I believe that what happened to me on Everest was a fluke—not something I would expect to happen again—and it hasn't scared me away. Since coming home, I've led groups up Mount Rainier, Mount Baker, Mount Shuksan, and other Cascade peaks. I've also climbed Vinson Massif in Antarctica and soloed Mount Aconcagua in the Andes mountains, which means I've soloed the summit of the highest peaks in both the Northern and the Southern Hemispheres.

I continue to climb for many reasons: because I love the outdoors, because I love being in God's creation, because I love the sense of accomplishment that comes from achieving a challenging goal, and because it fits the way I've been wired—physically, emotionally, and spiritually. And perhaps most of all, I climb because I love sharing outdoor adventures with other people, helping open their eyes to the awe I have experienced myself at high places.

•

One year after my summit, JoAnna planned a family picnic at a park near our home with a great view of Mount Si, Mount Baker, and the Cascades. I'm not the type who likes days that are all about me—I'd rather celebrate other people's special occasions and fly under the radar for "Brian days"—so I was glad this was low key, a special moment to spend with my three favorite people in the world.

The kids had grown a lot in the past year, and they'd gotten used to Daddy being a topic of conversation in the media and on TV. But they didn't see anything different about me—to them I was still just Daddy.

That day we went on a nature hike and then ate lunch. JoAnna explained to the kids why the day was special, but we didn't go into much detail about it. After our picnic, I lay on the blanket, taking in the moment and hugging my kids until they broke loose to chase bugs. In my mind, I drifted back to my accomplishment on Everest and everything I'd endured a year before. Knowing the other scenarios that could have happened, I felt so blessed to be there with my family in that moment.

When I recalled being in my office recording that good-bye message for my family before I left, I never could have predicted what lay ahead and how God would work. I felt truly blessed that JoAnna and the kids never had to sit through that video.

This is what JoAnna wrote, reflecting on the one-year anniversary of my summit.

May 15, 2012

Today we celebrated that Brian is home and safe with us one year after Everest. I planned a family picnic at Snoqualmie Point Park. It was a simple thing, but it was so nice to be in the sun together, enjoying a meal as a family. I'm so thankful for all that Brian has accomplished, but even more important, I'm thankful he is alive and here with us.

Looking back, I can't believe all we've been through. If I'd known ahead of time what Brian would have to endure on Everest, I never would have agreed for him to go. But despite all the challenges we faced during and after the climb, I wouldn't change anything. Our faith grew tremendously through this experience, and now we know that with faith, anything is possible. We have seen God's faithfulness firsthand.

I am amazed at the way God works and how Brian's story continues to reach so many people in different ways. It has been a blessing to hear him tell his story, emotional as it is. We have both worked at overcoming our fears—he even went back to climbing that same year. Brian amazes me in so many ways, but I'm even more amazed at the way God has worked in both of us through this and the story he has given us to share.

•

If there's one question I've gotten more than any other since returning from Everest, it's this one: "Did you make it to the top?"

And while that's a worthwhile question, it's not the ultimate one. Summit or not, there's so much more that goes into a big goal like this one. As with any aspiration in life, you get more out of the knowledge and experience you gain along the way than you do from that moment of completion. In many ways I returned from my Everest expedition the same man I was before I left. But in other ways, I'll never be the same again.

I always knew that I was physically and mentally tough, but you don't know how tough you really are until you're put to the test. I never would have chosen to go through something like this, but it was gratifying to get to the other side and know I'd passed. I learned that I can be determined and focused enough to fight for survival in a crisis situation.

One of the biggest changes in my life after Everest has been a deeper faith in God. For much of my life, I've taken credit for my own accomplishments (whether that was legitimate or not), but I don't deserve any of the honor for what happened at 27,500 feet. I was given life and energy that I didn't have in reserve. I can't take credit for what happened in that moment—it wasn't from me, and it wasn't from this world.

Another way my life has changed since climbing Everest is that I've been given chances to share about Christ as I tell my story. I've always been pretty private about my faith—not that I kept it hidden, but I certainly never had the opportunity to talk about a miracle of Christ onstage, on the radio, on social media, or on TV. I've been interviewed by people who weren't coming from a religious perspective, but I can't tell my story without including the parts about how God worked. So whether I'm talking to a group of 30 people or a crowd of 70,000, I always share the whole story.

I've accomplished something that the majority of people have never experienced, let alone imagined, and my body and my mind have endured something that nobody else on record has ever accomplished. Most people don't get the specifics of my journey, but then again, they've climbed mountains of their own that I can't fathom.

Whether your mountain is a literal one or not, I believe that God has put each of us on this planet to live a life that is beyond imagination. I don't recommend the death zone for everyone, but I do recommend that whatever spot you find yourself in, you discover and climb your personal Mount Everest.

Maybe for you the goal is running a 5K after years of saying you can't run. Or maybe you want to get into good enough shape to play with your kids or grandkids. Or perhaps your battle is more of an internal one—you want to heal a fractured relationship, or you're trying to overcome mental and emotional damage you've been carrying with you since childhood.

Whatever your mountain is—no matter how impossible it seems at times, no matter how many obstacles you face along the way, and no matter how many people tell you it can't be done—it is possible for you to summit.

My parting words are simple: live life. Create goals, and then chase after them. When you do, be aware of your surroundings and be prepared to alter your goals when un-expected changes come up. Don't be afraid to fail, and always keep the faith. Whatever it is God has put on your heart to accomplish, I encourage you to push your limits—you never know what you're truly capable of, and you may just surprise yourself.

When you get discouraged along the way, take confi-dence in these words from Scripture: "Humanly speaking, it is impossible. But not with God. Everything is possible with God" (Mark 10:27, NLT).

And when people ask you if you made it to the top, remind yourself that summit or not, that's not the most important thing. The most important thing is who you are becoming along the way.

So when people ask me if I summited Mount Everest, my response is simple. I tell them, "I survived."

ACKNOWLEDGMENTS

I'M SO GRATEFUL for my wife, JoAnna, who puts up with me every day. She is truly a wonderful wife, mother, and best friend (and she is also superhot). Without her, I would be nothing. My children, Emily and Jordan, are my strength and my motivation during times of struggle. I am so blessed to have them in my life, and I cherish every day I'm able to witness their spiritual and emotional growth.

I'm thankful for my time in the US Navy and the extensive training I went through to become an air rescue swimmer. The Aircrew, AIRR, and SERE instructors were tough, but they made me tough, and I credit them with preparing me to do what it took to stay alive and never consider quitting. I also want to thank those who have served our great country to ensure our continued safety and freedom.

During my expedition, I witnessed the remarkable effects of the power of prayer. Church on the Ridge is filled with amazing people, and I'm so thankful for the prayers they offered when I was in need. I want to give special thanks to Pastor Charlie Salmon, who gave me a much-needed mental boost halfway through my journey when I Skyped him from base camp.

Funding a mountaineering hobby can't be done alone—not for me, at least. I couldn't ask for cooler sponsors than Presidio, partnering with Cisco Systems, NetApp, and VMware. They helped make my dream a reality. I'd also like to thank Cisco Systems for supporting my unpaid time off to climb. It's great to see a major company that puts a priority on living out your dreams.

I also want to give recognition to my Sherpa crew, who were some of the most selfless people I've had the pleasure to meet. I have a lifelong friend in Pasang, and I feel confident I'll see the rest of the team in the future. I also want to give thanks to the team that helped coordinate this life-changing experience for me.

I want to acknowledge several people who made *Blind Descent* possible. First, thanks to my close friend Tony Russell, whose prayers and personal connections helped me develop some important relationships. Thanks to Scott Brickell for inviting me into his home to share my story with his wonderful family in Franklin, Tennessee, and for his warm introductions to specific folks in the entertainment industry. It was cool to be backstage with the Rock and Worship Roadshow bands and have the chance to share my Everest experience with MercyMe before they hit the stage—especially since their music was an inspiration for me during the actual climb.

I'd like to extend a huge thanks to Bill Reeves and the Working Title Agency for the friendship they have brought to me and my family. Bill is the real deal, and he spreads the word about Christ through the unique stories of others.

I owe a special bit of gratitude to the professionals at

Tyndale House Publishers. I'm sure I drove Carol and Stephanie crazy with my straight-to-the-point personality and my constant humor. I put utter importance in maintaining my voice throughout my writing, and Tyndale always respected my wishes without trying to change who I am. I couldn't ask for better publishers or editors.

And most important, I want to thank our Creator for watching over my family while I was gone, for giving me the strength and ability to achieve great heights, and for delivering me from almost certain death on the top of the world.

NOTES

CHAPTER 1: EXPEDITION OF A LIFETIME

1. Nick Heil, "The Worst Disasters on Everest," *Outside Online*, April 26, 2012, http://www.outsideonline.com/outdoor-adventure/climbing/mountaineering /everest-2012/The-Worst-Disasters-on-Everest-1-1996.html.
2. Ashley Strickland, "Everest Climbers, Widower Recount Deadly Traffic Jam on Top of the World," CNN, May 28, 2013, http://www.cnn.com/2013 /05/25/travel/everest-2012-anniversary.
3. Jesse Greenspan, "7 Things You Should Know about Mount Everest," History .com, May 29, 2013, http://www.history.com/news/7-things-you-should -know-about-mount-everest.

CHAPTER 2: THE LONG ROAD TO NEPAL

1. Brian Dickinson, "Brian Dickinson: Reader Blog 2," *Climbing*, April 1, 2011, http://www.climbing.com/climber/brian-dickinson-reader-blog-2.

CHAPTER 4: INTO THICK AIR

1. Brian Dickinson, "Brian Dickinson: Reader Blog 8," *Climbing*, April 14, 2011, http://www.climbing.com/climber/brian-dickinson-reader-blog-8.

CHAPTER 5: LIFE AT ALTITUDE

1. Brian Dickinson, "Brian Dickinson: Reader Blog 14," *Climbing*, April 28, 2011, http://www.climbing.com/climber/brian-dickinson-reader-blog-14.

CHAPTER 8: DESCENDING ON FAITH

1. Taken from Dennis Broadwell, "Everest Expedition 2011 with Mountain Gurus: Final Dispatch #25," *Mountain Gurus* (blog), May 22, 2011, http:// mountaingurus.blogspot.com/2011/05/mountain-gurus-everest-expedition -2011_22.html.

CHAPTER 9: ESCAPING THE DEATH ZONE

1. Brian Dickinson, "Brian Dickinson: Reader Blog 16," *Climbing*, May 17, 2011, http://www.climbing.com/climber/brian-dickinson-reader-blog-16.

ABOUT THE AUTHOR

BRIAN DICKINSON served for six years as a US Navy air rescue swimmer before he moved to the Pacific Northwest to get his MBA and pursue his passion for extreme sports and mountain climbing. He has climbed in expeditions on the highest peaks of the seven continents, including Mount Everest, with the majority of climbs in the Cascade mountains, near his home. He uses his climbs to help raise money for charity and as an opportunity to share his faith with others around the world. Brian, his wife, JoAnna, and their children, Jordan and Emily, live in Snoqualmie, Washington.